The Age of the Common School, 1830-1865

Studies in the History of American Education Series

Henry J. Perkinson and Vincent P. Lannie

General Editors

Sheldon Cohen
A History of Colonial Education, 1607–1776

David Madsen
Early National Education, 1776–1830

Frederick M. Binder
The Age of the Common School, 1830–1865

Patricia Albjerg Graham
Community and Class in American Education, 1865–1918

Edgar Gumbert and Joel H. Spring
The Superschool and the Superstate:
American Education in the Twentieth Century, 1918–1970

The Age of the Common School, 1830-1865

Frederick M. Binder

City College of New York

John Wiley & Sons, Inc., New York · London · Sydney · Toronto

Library of Congress Cataloging in Publication Data:

Binder, Frederick M
   The age of the common school, 1830–1865.

   (Studies in the history of American education series)
   Bibliography: p.
   1. Education—United States—History. I. Title.

LA208.B56 1974   370′.973   73–22214
ISBN 0-471-07312-1
ISBN 0-471-07313-X (pbk.)

Printed in the United States of America

10 9 8 7 6 5 4 3 2 1

For Abby

series preface

This series provides new interpretations of American educational history based on the best recent scholarship. It contains five volumes that present, chronologically and topically, the history of American education from the beginning to the present day.

Each volume gives an original analysis and interpretation of the development of formal and informal agencies of education during a particular period.

Henry J. Perkinson

contents

The Age of the Common School, 1830-1865

chapter one
a climate for reform

the term "Age of the Common School" has been popularly given to the 35 years preceding the end of the Civil War during which there occurred a largely successful campaign to attain free, universal, public schooling on the elementary level. Historians enjoy grouping years together and assigning to them dramatic and catchy titles. With the 1830s, 1840s, and 1850s the chroniclers had a field day. In addition to "The Age of the Common School" we have, within this period, "The Era of Reform," "Antebellum America," "The Age of Jackson," and "The Era of Expansion," not to mention, in the field of educational history alone, "The Age of the Academy" and "The Era of the College." These and other names have been attached to the various manifestations of an American nation in its period of exuberant adolescence. Its independence and sense of nationhood apparently secure, and its political institutions established, the United States, at the outset of the second quarter of the nineteenth century, embarked on an era of sudden and rapid physical and economic growth that transformed not only the face of the nation but, to a large extent, its mind and spirit as well.

We who live in the midst of a technological civilization witness the harnessing of the atom or the conquest of outer space with little more than a nod. Such feats seem less miraculous when they come one after another over a period of several generations. But consider for a moment the reactions of men when what has been the same for centuries is transformed so completely within a lifetime. In America, during the period under consideration, such change occurred in transportation, communications, settlement of the land, manufacturing, modes of power, and in man's very conception of himself in relation to his fellow men, his creator, and the universe. Wherever we look during these years we observe dramatic movement and rapid change. "Our population is destined to roll its resistless wastes to the icy barriers of the north, and to encounter Oriental civilization on the shores of the Pacific," wrote William Seward in 1846, and before the decade was over the Southwest and Pacific Coast were ours. Between 1830 and 1860 the United States added 1,234,566 square miles of territory. Room was provided, and the population grew—from 12,866,020 in 1830 to 31,443,321 in 1860. Between 1830 and 1840 Indiana's population doubled and that of Illinois tripled. To bind the nation together came the canals and then the railroads—23 miles of track in 1830, 30,626 miles by 1860. Shortly after the first telegraph link was established between Baltimore and Washington in 1844, Morse's wires crisscrossed the entire nation.

The opening and settlement of vast tracts of land in the West guaranteed continued agricultural expansion. Census reports throughout this period—indeed through 1910—confirm the fact that the majority of Americans lived in rural areas. The American frontier continued, for many years, to exert a significant impact on the nation's economic development, continued to foster democratic tendencies, and continued to represent a beacon of hope for those who desired a better life:

> Come all ye Yankee farmers who wish to
> change your lot,
> Who've spunk enough to travel beyond your
> native spot,

And leave behind the village where Pa and
    Ma do stay,
Come follow me and settle in Michigania,—
Yea, yea, yea, in Michigania!

But the census figures of these decades reveal another pattern of population movement and growth even more dramatic and, in the long run, more significant than that of the westward flow of agricultural settlement. Commencing in the 1820s, and increasing in intensity in the 1830s, 1840s, and 1850s, America experienced the beginning of its unceasing march toward the urban-industrial nation it has now become. In 1820 only 7.2 percent of the population lived in urban areas (2500 people or more); by 1860 the figure had risen to 20 percent. Whereas, during each of these decades, the total national population increased by one-third, urban population rose by nearly 90 percent. The United States in 1860 could boast of 101 cities with populations over 10,000. Forty years earlier there had been only 12. Of the 101, 8 had passed the 100,000 mark, and the population of New York City, when combined with the then independent Brooklyn, exceeded 1 million. The growth of New York, Philadelphia, Baltimore, and other eastern port cities was phenomenal. Equally impressive was the appearance of new urban centers in the West. As a number of historians have recently pointed out, the urban impulse played no small role in the westward movement. Several river cities, including Pittsburgh, St. Louis, Detroit, and Cincinnati, were founded prior to any significant agricultural settlement in their vicinity.

As the cities of America grew in number, they also improved and expanded their functions. The location of the older centers on ocean harbors and at strategic points along navigable inland waterways bespoke a primary concern with commercial trade. The inception of canals, steamboats, and railroads proved a boon to American commerce. To the urban centers of the East came the foodstuffs of the West and the cotton of the South. On the return trips went the tools, finished textiles, and luxury items of an industrial economy. Traditionally the Eastern cities had served as stopover warehouses, storing and then shipping the raw materials and farm produce of the land to Europe, receiving and merchandising the finished goods of Old World factories. However, when the embargo and War of 1812 virtually shut off trade with Europe, American commercial capital was channeled into new ventures in home-grown industry. Factories appeared in the older cities, and new urban settlements sprouted by the river falls of New England to serve as mill towns for the production of cotton and, after 1840, wool cloth. This flowering of American industry during the Jacksonian period was aided by a significant spurt in technology. Yankee ingenuity produced new power looms, carding machines, the vulcanization of rubber, improvements in printing, the telegraph, advances in metal fabrication, and numerous other inventions and refinements.

Complementing the movement to the agrarian West was the gradual emergence of a city-bound migration of sons and daughters of farm families for whom urban life held an even greater attraction than virgin land. The news of opportunity reached beyond America's rural farms and villages. "*Amerika, du hast es besser*," wrote Goethe in 1831, and thousands of Europeans crossed the Atlantic, half a million between 1830 and 1840 and then, beginning in the late 1840s, over 200,000 a year. For the first time non-English immigrants predominated, with Irish and Germans each more numerous than those coming from America's mother country. Significantly, where most newcomers traditionally sought their fortunes in the soil, a large number of Germans and a vast majority of the Irish settled in the cities.

The great expansion of industrial and agricultural productivity and the dramatic swiftness with which the nation's boundaries moved westward surely matched the most ambitious dreams of the Founding Fathers. But the American Revolution had promised to show the world more than the possibility of colonies gaining independence from a powerful mother country, more than a raw frontier land transformed into a

prosperous nation. Young America had declared itself the proving grounds of the Enlightenment. Here, the belief that the
democratic mass of people applying the force of reason could
attain the best of all societies would be tested. After delays
brought about by the conservative retrenchment of the Federalist years and the dislocations of a second war with Britain,
the election of Andrew Jackson signaled the culmination of the
American Revolution as a social movement. During the 1830s
the Jacksonian party formed a coalition of Southern yeomen
and small planters, frontier settlers, Irish and German immigrants, and urban workers and proudly adopted the label
"Democrat." As for their generally more conservative Whig
opponents, by 1840 most of them were quite ready to identify
with democracy and, indeed, to insist that their man Harrison
was of the people while Jackson's successor, Van Buren, was a
champagne-drinking aristocrat:

> Let Van from his coolers of silver drink wine,
>> And lounge on his cushioned settee;
> Our man on his buckeye bench can recline
>> Content with hard cider is he!

One might speculate as to the reasons why the more conservative, more prosperous, better-educated Whigs who had
been so repulsed by the sight of the mobs that had flocked to
Jackson's 1829 inaugural should, a few years later, proclaim
such democratic sentiments. Of one thing there is no doubt:
no party in 1840 could ignore the masses and hope to win the
presidency. In 1824 only 356,038 Americans had voted for the
president. Four years later the figure increased by 224 percent
to 1,155,340. Two factors were most responsible for the change.
First, the Federalist plan to restrict the selection of presidential electors to the members of the state legislatures was overturned in state after state, and this power was handed to the
electorate. By 1832 only South Carolina continued the older
practice. Even more significant were advances in the direction

of universal manhood suffrage. By the 1820s the highly restrictive property requirements began to give way to a more liberal low-tax qualification. Next was the removal of all restrictions, a step taken by Vermont and New Hampshire as early as the 1790s. By 1850 twenty-seven states had adopted universal manhood suffrage, six had a small tax qualification, and only North Carolina continued to maintain a significant property requirement. Who but perhaps a handful of abolitionists and feminists would then challenge Tocqueville's statement, written over a decade earlier, that "the principle of the sovereignty of the people has acquired in the United States all the practical development that the imagination can conceive"?

As the United States moved into the 1830s the religious beliefs and practices of her people mirrored much that was inherent in the movement to democratize politics. If the cool, rationalistic religion of the New England Unitarian appears at first glance to have nothing in common with the evangelistic faith of the foot-stomping frontier farmer at his camp meeting, then a second look is necessary. Because, although the Unitarian placed his trust in reason to guide him to salvation while the Baptist, Methodist, or member of one of the numerous other Protestant sects stressed such things as conversion, acceptance of Jesus, and the renouncing of sin, all were fundamentally optimistic in their belief that man and his world were indeed capable of salvation. The dominant mood of the day rejected the Calvinistic conceptions of a world hopelessly bound in sin and of a totally depraved mankind just as it rejected religious and political rule by a self-proclaimed elite.

America moved forward, during these years, with seemingly boundless energy and an optimism tempered by certain anxieties. It was not, by any means, an age free of problems. The growth of cities brought to the nation the first symptoms of the urban malaise we know so well today: substandard housing, congestion, disease, and inadequate sanitation and transportation facilities. The waves of immigrants, including the first substantial influx of Roman Catholics, appeared to many to represent cheap competition for jobs and to others a potential threat to the stability of the American way of life and system of beliefs. The rapid growth of industry and commerce did not occur without dislocations. The year 1837 saw the land engulfed in a most serious depression. As business activity became more intense and complex, there were losers as well as winners in the race for prosperity. And those most sensitive to the shortcomings of society could not ignore the persistent presence of war, slavery, disease, and the manifold inequities of class, race, and sex. Yet, in an era when many believed fervently in the ability of human effort to overcome all obstacles, problems such as these were accepted with seeming enthusiasm as challenges and as opportunities for men to prove the validity of their faith in themselves, their nation, and its institutions. In such a climate America's first great era of social reform was born. Doubt and pessimism were in full retreat, turning to counterattack only as time approached Charleston harbor and the guns of Fort Sumter.

The movement to improve the quality of the free public schools where they existed and to extend them to areas where they did not was but one of many ventures in reform. In addition there were organized efforts to further such causes as the temperance crusade, the abolition of slavery, world peace, improved prison conditions, women's rights, and more humane treatment of the poor, the blind, and the insane. With the exception of women's rights, the leaders of these causes were, at the time of their involvement, usually not victims of the evils they sought to remove. Instead, most were men and women of the middle class, moderately to well-educated and firm in their belief in the brotherhood of man and the fatherhood of God. Although there were among them men active in politics and participants in government, and although they often sought legislative action in behalf of their causes, their efforts were primarily directed through nonpartisan organizations, and in their appeals they avoided party labels. To these people the conditions they sought to remedy were associated with injus-

tice and immorality. Holding fast to their convictions, like their
Puritan forebears, they would not and they could not be de-
tracted from their course. The price of failure was the end of
their dreams of the good society, which they were absolutely
convinced their particular brand of reform could achieve.
While the focus of this book is on educational reform, we cannot forget the other causes. For there were few reform movements whose leaders failed to acknowledge the potential value
of the public schools as vehicles for the promotion of their
objectives, and there were few educational advocates who
failed to envision their cause as the key to all reform.

The common-school movement was initiated and led by men
who were dissatisfied with the quality of and opportunities for
education in their states. As the era of egalitarianism opened,
the nation's pattern of elementary schooling seemed ill-equipped
either to prepare children to reap the fruits of promised opportunities or to meet the responsibilities of citizenship in a society whose goal was to be no less than a model of enlightened
democracy, economic well-being, and Christian morality. But
the reformers were motivated by more than their conviction
that education was crucial in attaining the American dream.
Although fundamentally optimistic in their outlook, they, too,
were concerned that certain economic, political, and social
developments of their day might lead to a future far from
glorious. Could not the newly enfranchised masses bring with
them mob rule similar to the bloody days of the French Revolution? Was it beyond the realm of possibility that the waves
of Irish Catholic and German immigrants just beginning to
flow into the country might prove dangerous to American institutions? What threats to the general welfare of the nation
might the growing, unpropertied, working class represent;
and, on the other side of the coin, what of those few to whom
the industrial age was bringing immense wealth and economic
power? To counter such dangers the reformers placed great
faith in a system of schooling in which children from all
classes, from all walks of life, together, and in *common* would

be exposed to the rudiments of learning and the virtues of patriotism and morality. There was cause for hope that in such an environment social order and mutual respect among classes could be fostered.

Although school reformers throughout the nation joined in common cause, the obstacles they encountered varied from state to state and from region to region. While avoiding unnecessary repetition of material found in other volumes of this series, we briefly examine here the status of public elementary education at the outset of the Age of the Common School. In New England a system of public education had been established as early as the seventeenth century. There, colonial governments responded to the desire of the established and highly influential Puritan clergy that all children be educated primarily to ensure that they be orthodox in the faith.[1] There, also, the concentration of population in towns and villages facilitated school organization. However, by 1830, although the principle of publicly supported and controlled education continued to be accepted in theory, the system had eroded.

Among the factors responsible for the educational decline was the diminishing power of the clergy. Developments in Massachusetts were typical of the region. In that state ministers had once been charged by law to join the town selectmen in governing the community's school system. But the nationwide trend to separate church from state was to alter this arrangement. By 1827, six years before the complete disestablishment of the Congregationalist Church in Massachusetts, effective control of school matters was totally in the hands of popularly elected school committees. The state government had relegated to the clergy only the responsibility for encouraging school attendance by children of their congregations. While one may applaud this action as a victory of the Enlightenment, in New England it had the effect of depriving the schools of

[1] Rhode Island, lacking the moral suasion and political influence of Puritan divines, was an exception to the New England pattern of education.

the direct involvement of an extremely effective and concerned group of men.

Also detrimental to the strength of the public school system was voluntary dispersal of the population once the Indian threat had been removed. The difficulties involved in sending children from scattered farm settlements to distant town schools were recognized by the legislature in the late eighteenth and early nineteenth centuries. Towns were empowered to decentralize their school system through the establishment of school districts whose governing bodies would share powers and responsibilities with the towns' school committees. While we may once more see a victory for democracy in the establishment of local school districts, this action, as with the weakening of clerical influence, had an adverse effect on the quality of education.

The frontier that fostered egalitarian and individualistic sentiments also tended to breed negative attitudes toward "book larnin" as a symbol of useless and effete aristocratic pretentiousness. In Massachusetts and other New England states, rural residents reflected this spirit in a reluctance to tax themselves beyond a bare minimum. This resulted in the fewest possible months in the school calendar, a minimal number of years of schooling for the children, pitifully low salaries for teachers, and inadequate physical facilities. As the schools deteriorated, those who were concerned for the educational welfare of their children, and who could afford to, turned more and more to private institutions. This was an alarming phenomenon to the friends of public education. Parents who invested their money in private school tuition were likely to be as opposed to supporting increased school taxes as the apathetic farmer. Lack of confidence in the town schools was bound to result in their eventual emergence as institutions serving the poor exclusively. Massachusetts pioneer school reformer James Carter in 1826 predicted that, if the tide of decay was not stemmed, the public schools would be extinct in 20 years. Only by improving the quality of public school education could confidence be restored and the town schools become common in fact as well as in name.

Despite these problems the New England states were the envy of school reformers throughout the nation. The principle of free, tax-supported public education, whose roots were firmly established in Yankee soil by the end of the eighteenth century, was still a primary goal in the rest of the nation at the beginning of the Jacksonian period. Perhaps the most promising picture was provided by developments in New York. There, education-conscious settlers among westward migrating New Englanders were instrumental in challenging the established tradition of tuition-supported private and religious education for the privileged and charity schooling sponsored by philanthropic agencies for the poor. By 1830 a series of legislative enactments had established a system of public elementary education with responsibility for control, supervision, and funding divided among the state government, towns, and school districts. However, the schools were not entirely free. The employment of funds raised by district taxation was restricted by law to meeting the costs of physical facilities and their maintenance. The monies received from town and state were usually inadequate to cover the remaining educational expenses, particularly teachers' salaries. To raise additional funds, districts were authorized to employ the rate-bill device, which placed an additional tax on each family based on the number of children enrolled in the public schools and the number of days in attendance. This amounted, in fact, to a tuition charge for each child. While parents who could not afford these payments were excused, they and their children were forced to bear the label of charity cases. Many chose to keep their children at home rather than accept such status. The rate-bill thus became a primary target of New York school reformers throughout the 1830s and 1840s. Obtaining its elimination was not to be an easy task. By means of this device a significant share of educational costs were met. In 1831, out of a total teachers' salary expenditure of $586,520, $346,807 was raised through the rate-bill. Legislators were none too eager to lift this burden from the backs of parents and place it on the general taxpaying public. The citizens of New York would first have to be convinced that their welfare and that of the state was dependent on the education of other people's children.

This description of events in New York State must be amended in order to consider conditions in New York City, which had been permitted to follow a separate course of educational development. In the city a clear division between schooling for the poor and the economically self-sufficient persisted. While the latter sent their children to private schools usually sponsored by religious bodies, a completely distinct system of charity schools run by the nongovernmental Public School Society received most of the city's share of the state common-school fund. Though the Society tried nobly to fulfill its self-assigned mission of providing free schooling "in the city of New York for the education of such children as do not belong to, or are not provided for, by any religious society," the task was overwhelming. In 1829, already forced to charge a small tuition fee, the Society declared that there were, in the city, 24,200 children between 5 and 15 who were not attending school. Their schools, they estimated, enrolled approximately 10,000 children compared with 17,500 in the several private institutions. The existence of large numbers of unschooled children in the city can be explained partly by the financial inability of the Society to accommodate them all and partly by the difficulties of parents in accumulating even the small tuition fee required for entry into the Society's schools. But there is also evidence that many of New York City's poor exhibited the same reluctance to declare a need for charity as did their upstate brethren. The Society itself was ready to pronounce, in 1829, "that these schools should be supported from public revenue, should be public property, and should be open to all, not as charity, but as a matter of common right."

Moving down the coast, an examination of the educational scene in Pennsylvania will provide a general idea of conditions in New Jersey, Maryland, and Delaware as well. As late as 1790 the Constitution of Pennsylvania had decreed that the state's role in education was to be limited to providing schools where "the poor may be taught gratis." From earliest colonial times education on both tuition and charity bases had been provided by the several religious sects with which Pennsylvania was more than abundantly blessed. As time passed, these groups stubbornly and effectively resisted attempts to set up a competing public school system. By the end of 1810, the legislature had gone only as far as providing financial assistance for the education of children whose parents were willing to declare themselves indigent. Thus publicly supported education became clearly associated with pauperism, which made it as much an anathema to the ruggedly proud and independent western farmers as to the eastern Quakers and German pietists who owed their allegiance to sectarian schools.

With the exception of Philadelphia, Lancaster, and Pittsburgh, where special state laws had helped institute effective public charity school systems, public education in Pennsylvania hardly existed in 1830. In 1824 an act had been pushed through the legislature that sought to provide "more effectually for the education of the poor gratis, and for laying the foundation of a general system of education throughout the Commonwealth." This merely permitted communities who so desired to erect a public school system and to tax themselves for its support. Yet, even this was too much for the opponents of public education. The act was repealed in 1826. The task ahead for Pennsylvania advocates of the common school was immense.

Clement Eaton in his book *The Freedom-of-Thought Struggle in the Old South* (Durham, North Carolina, 1940) entitled one of his chapters "The Dark Cloud of Illiteracy." In it he provides considerable evidence to support his description of the sad state of popular education in the South. A few examples will suffice. In 93 counties of Virginia in 1818, 4682 people applied for marriage licenses, of whom 1127 could not sign their names. In a contested congressional election in North Carolina in 1831, of 111 voters who gave testimony, 28 made their mark, an indication of their inability to write their names. A committee of the Louisiana legislature in 1831 reported that, of approximately 9000 white children in the state between 10 and 15, "not one third of that number received any instruction whatever."

Little change had occurred in Southern education since the colonial period. Men of means had their children tutored at home or sent to private schools. Children of the poor had no choice but to rely on the limited facilities provided by philanthropy. In the most rural parts of this rural region, in the western sections of the upper South and throughout the lower South, educational opportunities for the masses were nearly totally absent.

The concept of public education was by no means alien to the Southern mind. There were still men who cherished Jefferson's dream of a complete system of tax-supported public schooling from the elementary level through the university. Ironically, this area that so neglected public common schooling was a leader in founding state universities. Georgia, in 1785, had the distinction of being the first state to charter a public college. However, without at the same time providing facilities to prepare talented youngsters from all sectors of society for admission, one can hardly conclude that "public" in this case implied a significant growth of democratic opportunity.

Events in the South prior to 1830 indicate that while, as might be expected, the powerful planter interests were not inclined to sponsor the growth of democracy through public education, neither were the nonslaveholding yeomanry particularly enthusiastic about initiating schooling or taxing themselves for its support. Two examples of efforts to foster public elementary schooling are illustrative of the Southern mood. Virginia had, since 1818, maintained a state literary fund for the purpose of supporting the education of poor children through grants for tuition, books, and supplies—a system of public philanthropy. Largely as a result of efforts by representatives of the small-farm western counties, a bill was passed in 1829 that enabled any district that so chose to use its portion of the literary fund to establish a "free school for the instruction, without fee or reward, to every white child within said district." The act accomplished little. Neither East nor West responded to the call for local initiative.

Turning to the second example, South Carolina in 1811 passed legislation directed toward encouraging free schools. Rather than calling for local tax support, the law authorized a state appropriation of $300 each for the support of a number of schools equal to the total membership of the lower chamber of the state legislature. These schools were to be open free to all white children, but if the funds proved inadequate to the demand, poor children were to be given preference. This law was in effect in 1830, but a combination of planter hostility and rural apathy had resulted in minimal efforts to carry out its provisions. Neither Virginia nor South Carolina really proved exceptions to the generally gloomy conditions that confronted Southern proponents of the common school at the outset of the Jacksonian Era.

By 1830 three of the five states that were to be carved out of the Northwest Territory had been admitted to the Union: Ohio, Indiana, and Illinois. Into the Territory had poured settlers from New England, the Middle Atlantic states, and the upper South, bringing with them values, beliefs, and institutions to be planted in the new soil. In terms of education, this meant that there were present in each of the recently created states advocates of the various patterns of school sponsorship and control we have observed in the older sections of the nation: public, private, religious, and philanthropic. Also present was a heaping dose of frontier attitudes toward schooling, ranging from apathy to outright antagonism. The fact is that the proponents of the common school in the Midwest were forced to overcome hostility emanating from two very different sources. On one hand there were the relatively affluent citizens who sent their children to private schools or patronized the religious schools. They argued that public schools would impose upon them what amounted to a double tax and would force them to pay for the education of other men's children. On the other hand were the poor and uneducated frontier farmers of whom we have spoken. The attitudes of these people and their ability to block educational reform was aptly exhibited in Illinois during the late 1820s.

In 1825 the Illinois legislature passed a law declaring that "common...schools open to all white citizens between the ages of five and 21 should be established, and shall be free to all classes of such citizens." The law further provided for the establishment of school districts upon petition from area residents, local control in each district by an elected corporate body, and state financial assistance. A resident of the town of Jacksonville recalled the response to the legislature's action:

I well remember the opposition there was to this school law on the part of the poor people, who feared that their children would be educated and wholly unfitted for work on the farm; the very class which the law was intended to benefit opposed it most bitterly.

The legislative session of 1826–1827, as historian John Pulliam writes, "cut the heart of the law and reduced it to the mere shadow of its original form." In its new shape the school law permitted voters to determine whether to maintain schools through the subscription of their patrons, through full tax support, or through partial tax support with parents making up the difference by means of what amounted to a rate-bill. The ability of any district to provide free, tax-supported education was essentially destroyed by the law's provision that "No person shall hereafter be taxed for the support of any free school in this state unless by his own free will and consent, first had and obtained in writing." As Professor Pulliam concludes, "Thus the free school provisions which seemed a

'Yankee device' to many earlier settlers and politicians were stripped of their power to change the course of Illinois."

J. P. Foote, writing in 1855, described educational attitudes in Ohio during the early decades of the nineteenth century:

The early immigrants to Ohio from New England considered schools and churches among their first wants ... those from Pennsylvania considered them last ... while those from New Jersey, and the few from Maryland, Virginia, the other Southern states, had their views of education fixed upon so high a scale that nothing less than colleges, or seminaries of the highest class could claim much of their attention, or seem to require any extraordinary efforts for their establishment.

As a result of Yankee persistence and some skillful log rolling involving supporters of education and advocates of canal building, the cause of public schooling progressed in Ohio during the 1820s. A law passed in 1825 provided a solid foundation upon which to build a common-school system. Among its provisions were requirements for the compulsory establishment of school districts and county school taxes. Terms were included governing the distribution of funds from the sale of the school lands granted under the Land Ordinances of 1785 and 1787 and the Enabling Act under which Ohio entered the Union. The law also provided for teachers' examinations and a statewide prescribed curriculum of the three Rs.

The legislation of 1825 projected Ohio well ahead of her sister states of the old Northwest. However, there was still a long road to travel before even she could claim the existence of a statewide system of free common schools. For one thing, a rate-bill arrangement persisted into the 1830s. Also, in the districts where New England settlers were not present in large numbers, hostile citizens had little difficulty preventing the establishment of public schools. Frederick Jackson Turner accurately described conditions at this point in history when he wrote of the Midwest as "too new a section to have developed educational facilities to any large extent." He went on to state that "The pioneers' poverty, as well as the traditions of the southern interior from which they so largely came discouraged extensive expenditures for public schooling."

As 1830 commenced, no state provided a system of free, public, elementary education of such quality to attract the confidence of all classes. No state was barren territory for common-school reform. However, as we have seen, probing actions had been initiated during the 1820s, with some limited success. The foundation for the great era of reform had been laid in every region. Organized efforts to propagandize and lobby for the cause had begun. The American Lyceum, founded in 1826, had the promotion of common schools as one of its prime objectives. Established that same year, the *American Journal of Education* added a significant voice for school reform. In 1827 the Pennsylvania Society for the Promotion of Public Schools was instituted, and in 1829 reformers meeting in Cincinnati organized the Western Academic Institute and Board of Education.

These years also witnessed the efforts of James G. Carter, a prototype of the men who were to be in the forefront of reform during the Age of the Common School. Beginning in 1821, through numerous newspaper articles and pamphlets, Carter lobbied for a truly common school, an institution for "the diffusion of knowledge through all classes of people." He clearly perceived and lucidly described the conditions in Massachusetts that inhibited the attainment of this goal: inefficient teachers, bad texts, excessive decentralization of school control and supervision, the growth of private institutions, and public apathy. Carter was particularly insistent that greater responsibility for public schooling must be borne by the state and towns:

If the State continues to relieve themselves of the troubles of providing for the instruction of the whole people, and to shift the responsibility upon the town, and the towns upon the dis-

tricts, and the districts upon the individuals, each will take care of himself and his own family as he is able, and as he appreciates the blessings of a good education. The rich will, as a class, have much better instruction than they now have, while the poor will have much worse or none at all.

It was largely a result of Carter's efforts that the legislature in 1826 reduced the power of the districts by making the town school committees responsible for the certification and supervision of teachers. Not satisfied with this, he insisted that the great need was for the establishment of a statewide instrument of supervision, a state Board of Education. On this matter the Massachusetts legislature was not yet prepared to act. Nor was that body favorably disposed to his plea for a state teacher-training institution. In 1827 a bill incorporating the measure was defeated by a single vote in the upper house.

If Yankee reformers inherited anything from their Puritan ancestors, it was a conviction that their causes were absolutely just and a stubborn determination to see an idea through. Far from acknowledging defeat, Carter went on, that very same year, to invest his personal funds in a teacher-training establishment in the town of Lancaster. Even after financial difficulties and the enmity of local residents forced the closing of this short-lived institution, Carter persisted. He continued his fight into the new decade, no longer as the almost lone agitator of the 1820s, but as one of the leaders of a movement that embraced some of the most prominent figures of society. The year 1830 found him in the forefront of a group of concerned citizens organizing the American Institute of Instruction. The crusade had really just begun.

chapter two
_____
a crusade emerges

during the first half of the nineteenth century men of arts and letters delighted in proclaiming the uniqueness of America. They gloried in its people, its land, and its institutions. There was no doubt that we had already established the best system of government ever devised by man. Leadership in cultural creativity, they insisted, would surely be attained in a brief matter of time. Two passages of Walt Whitman's eloquently convey this mood:

> O hasten flag of man—O with sure and steady
>   step, passing highest flag of kings,
> Walk supreme to the heaven's mighty symbol—
>   run up above them all
> Flag of stars! thick-sprinkled bunting!
> . . . .
> Of all races and eras, These States, with
>   veins full of poetical stuff, most needs
>   poets, and are to have the greatest, and
>   use them the greatest,
> Their Presidents shall not be their common
>   referee so much as their poets shall.

Few Americans of this era would have hesitated to argue that decadent Europe had little for our new and vibrant nation to emulate. Yet, not only was it impossible—not to mention undesirable—to be culturally isolated, but in some respects we were still very much tied to mother Europe's apron strings. Our painters, architects, sculptors, poets, and authors, with few exceptions, slavishly copied European styles, and critics showed little tolerance for the works of those who did not. While reformers had their dreams firmly focused on the attainment of an American glory land, their eyes and ears were quick to respond to foreign developments that could prove fruitful at home. Several American reform movements had their counterparts in England and on the Continent. Ships plying the Atlantic carried both the leaders and the literature of causes— abolition, women's rights, international peace, labor, and education among them. Just as the writings of Locke and Rousseau had inspired Franklin, Jefferson, Rush, and other early advocates of a more egalitarian and utilitarian education, the works of nineteenth-century European educators and the educational reforms of European governments were to significantly influence American leaders of the common-school movement.

In the first ranks of men who have shaped the pattern of modern education stands Johann Heinrich Pestalozzi (1746– 1827). Sensitive to the destruction and upheavals suffered by his native Switzerland in the wake of Napoleon's invasion and internal political strife, Pestalozzi sought to establish moral order and social harmony through education. While by no means advocating the destruction of class divisions, he did believe that through schooling the children of the poor could be prepared to lead happy and fruitful lives. The influence of Locke and Rousseau is apparent in Pestalozzi's writings and in the curricula and methods he employed in his schools. He urged his teachers to view their pupils not as miniature adults but as children whose mental, moral, and physical development must be nurtured with tender care. Putting into practice what Rousseau had preached in the *Émile*, Pestalozzi attended

to the individual needs and interests of his students and sought
to create an environment conducive to the fullest development
of the natural talents of each child. He set aside the rod and
other devices of punishment and intimidation in favor of a
"thinking love," which stressed sympathy for the child and a
spirit of cooperation between teacher and learner. In addition
to recognizing the negative impact of fear on the learning process, Pestalozzi proclaimed the positive values of utilizing the
senses. His teachers were instructed to abandon the traditional
book-centered teaching methods in favor of techniques that
would correspond to children's natural inclination to learn
through the employment of their sensory organs. Furthermore,
he was convinced that subject matter could be presented in a
manner that paralleled the child's own development, beginning
with the rudiments and moving in a natural sequence to the
more complex.

Pestalozzi's teachers carried out his philosophy in their classrooms. Students learned through listening to the teacher and
observing and manipulating various man-made and natural objects that were both attractive and instructive. Under Pestalozzi's plan not only were the beauties and delights of nature
brought into the school, but the boundaries of the classroom
were broadened to include the surrounding woods and fields.

Pestalozzi's conception of education as preparation for life
led him to advocate an extension of the elementary school curriculum beyond the three Rs. In his early years of schoolkeep-
ing he sought to include agricultural and mechanical training
along with the more traditional subjects. Such activity he believed would help develop moral values, which he considered
natural by-products of proper work habits, and at the same
time prepare the youngsters physically and vocationally for
the responsibilities of adult life. In addition he had hopes of
aiding his school's treasury by creating a market for student
products. For various reasons, including the hostility of local
farmers and craftsmen, Pestalozzi was forced to abandon this
facet of his program. However, he did succeed in introducing

what were then considered novel subjects, such as music, geography, nature study, and drawing. These studies were considered particularly conducive to the harmonious development of the mental, moral, and physical faculties, which he viewed as the primary end of education.

One of Pestalozzi's most notable contributions was to broaden the concept of what constituted an able teacher. Under his system, mere mastery of subject matter and the ability to apply the rod no longer sufficed. His teachers were required through direct observation to understand the ways of children and to be responsible for their total development—social, physical, and emotional as well as intellectual. In addition to his other achievements, Pestalozzi must be cited as one of the earliest advocates and practitioners of professional training for teachers.

Pestalozzi's ventures attracted interest throughout the Western world. Visitors flocked to his schools and returned home with laudatory reports of his accomplishments. William Maclure, the Scottish-born American geologist and diplomat, paid a number of visits to Pestalozzi's school at Yverdon in 1804. So impressed was he with the Swiss master's methods that he invited Pestalozzi to come to the United States and establish a school in Philadelphia. Pestalozzi declined the offer but recommended a protegé, Joseph Neef. Neef arrived in Philadelphia in 1806 and joined Maclure in schemes to popularize Pestalozzian principles. That year Maclure published in the *National Intelligencer*, the first American account of Pestalozzi's activities. Two years later Neef published his treatise on Pestalozzianism, *Sketch of a Plan and Method of Education*. Further ventures by this pair in promoting educational reform ended ultimately in failure. Neef founded schools first in Philadelphia and Chester, Pennsylvania, and later in Louisville, Kentucky. These were short lived. Maclure, meanwhile, became interested in the social experiments of Robert Owen and the educational innovations of Philipp Emanuel von Fellenberg, who at Hofwyl in Switzerland conducted a school along Pestalozzian lines.

Among Fellenberg's students were the sons of Maclure and Owen. When Owen established his communal settlement at New Harmony, Indiana in 1825, Neef and Maclure were provided an exciting opportunity to direct its educational system, employing the principles and methods of the Swiss reformers. Unfortunately, within three years Owen's utopia was on the rocks. However, Owen's son Robert Dale moved on to other areas of reform, carrying with him an enthusiasm for the education he had experienced in Switzerland and Indiana.

William Maclure was the first American to visit Pestalozzi's school. Others followed and returned with equally glowing reports. John Griscom stopped at Yverdon in 1818. Americans reading his account of the visit were bound to be interested in ideas of a man of whom Griscom wrote, ". . . the period of his life and labors will, I fully believe, be hereafter regarded as a most important epoch in the history of education." William C. Woodbridge's favorable impressions of the work he observed at Yverdon were conveyed in his writings as editor of the *American Annals of Education*. He also authored textbooks (*Rudiments of Geography* in 1822 and *Universal Geography* in 1824) in which teaching techniques along lines recommended by Pestalozzi were employed.

Travel to Europe in search of educational ideas continued after Pestalozzi's death in 1827. Among the Americans touring the Continent in subsequent years were some of the leading figures of the common-school movement, including Horace Mann, Henry Barnard, and Calvin Stowe. Unlike their predecessors, these men received their most complete view of applied Pestalozzianism not in Switzerland but in Prussia. After suffering disastrous defeats at the hands of Napoleon's army in 1806–1807, Prussia's Frederick William III had decided to utilize the national educational system as a major element in a liberal political and social program for rebuilding the nation and assuring the patriotic support of its citizens. Urged on by the philosopher Fichte, Pestalozzianism was embraced, and beginning in 1808 prospective teachers were sent to Yverdon for their training. These young men subsequently returned to Prussia to practice in the schools and to instruct at the newly established teacher-training institutions. So complete was the conquest of Prussian elementary education by the Pestalozzian influence that one contemporary observer spoke of the "Prussian Pestalozzian school system" and declared of Pestalozzi, "Whatever of excellence or eminence they [the Prussian schools] have, they really owe to no one but to him."

Although the reaction that set in after the Congress of Vienna snapped the liberal spirit under which the educational reforms had been instituted, Prussia's schools continued to be models of efficient organization and Pestalozzian influence. So famous was this system that, when in 1836 the Ohio legislature commissioned Calvin Stowe to examine and report on European schools, it urged particular attention to the schools of Prussia.[1] In 1843 Horace Mann, responding to critics who insisted that Americans could learn little from studying the schools of so autocratic a state, declared:

If the Prussian schoolmaster has better methods of teaching reading, writing, grammar, geography, arithmetic, &c., so that, in half the time, he produces greater and better results, surely we may copy his modes of teaching those elements, without adopting his notions of passive obedience to government, or of blind adherence to the articles of a church.

Mann's report of his visit to Prussia confirmed the continuing influence of Pestalozzi's philosophy on school practices there:

1. During all this time, I never saw a teacher hearing a lesson

[1] Copies of Stowe's *Report on Elementary Instruction in Europe* were placed by the legislature in every school district in the state. Copies were ordered reprinted by the legislatures of Massachusetts, Pennsylvania, and Michigan.

of any kind (excepting reading or spelling) with a book in his hand.

2. *I never saw a teacher* sitting *while hearing a recitation.*

3. *Though I saw hundreds of schools, and thousands—I think I may say, within bounds, tens of thousands—of pupils,* I never saw one child undergoing punishment, or arraigned for misconduct. I never saw one child in tears from having been punished, or from fear of being punished.

American reformers found Europe fertile ground for material influential in shaping their own philosophy of education and useful in their campaign to win support for the common school. They were favorably impressed by the philosophy and methods of Pestalozzi and his followers. They envied the efficiency of the highly centralized educational systems of France and Prussia. But, as they crisscrossed Europe, they also found numerous examples of lands where education of the masses was sorely neglected, where ignorance seemed to breed poverty and the related threat of social upheaval. For example, Horace Mann, writing in the *Common School Journal* in 1844, described in vivid detail the vast gulf that separated the wealthy of England from the masses of working people dwelling in their squalid "hovels" and declared that the "source, origin, cause of all this is, the neglect of the masses by the possessors of wealth and of power;—mainly and primarily, the neglect of the education of the masses." Mann and his colleagues were quite aware that the shock value of such stories could be as effective a persuader as descriptions of educational achievements:

The moral we derive from these facts, in reference to our own country, is, the duty of every class of men, and of every individual man to do whatever in him lies for the welfare of the rising generation ... lest those terrible retributions, which God, by his eternal laws, has denounced against such offences, come also upon us. ... The common criminal has but two hands; the man who cherishes ignorance lifts many hands against his country.

The above words were written during the height of the campaign for common-school reform by the most outstanding leader of a band of respectable, influential reformers whose origins were solidly middle class. These were the men most responsible for the ultimate victory of the cause. But at the outset of our era, in 1830, there were men of a more radical stamp, acting from within a labor movement, who took the lead in pressing for universal, free, public education.

Beginning in Philadelphia in 1828, workingmen's parties were organized by craftsmen in nearly every city of the nation. Such action was in part an outgrowth of the extension of male suffrage and a vivid indication of faith in the power of the democratic political process. But it was also a consequence of some of the problems that were gradually emerging as by-products of an age of economic expansion. The advances in industry and commerce that contributed so much to the dynamic character of the era also brought, for many people, disruptions in a pattern of life that had formerly been quite secure and comfortable. The small shop with the master working in harmony alongside a few journeymen and apprentices had been a familliar and pleasant scene in America from its earliest days. However, the corporate form of ownership with its armies of anonymous investor-stockholders was proving far more suitable to the new conditions than the traditional proprietorship and partnership arrangements. A burgeoning economy was rapidly making the easy pace of the shop inefficient. Whether maintaining his own business or downgraded to the role of factory foreman, the master craftsman felt compelled by the demands of the market to work the journeyman to the limits during a working day that was often 12 hours long. The new developments in production, which made it more efficient to engage workers in the creation of parts of the finished goods, led to both lower wages and a deflation of pride in craft achievement. The very existence of the centuries-old apprentice system was endangered. There was a growing tendency to employ unskilled children, women and immigrants as cheap labor to man the new machines. The journeyman had been part of a ladder system of opportunity that enabled a young apprentice to realistically aspire to one day attain the position of master. He had held a respected place in society. Now, in this period of seemingly limitless opportunity, his status and his future appeared threatened.

In the face of such conditions the artisans organized for political action. They welcomed the support of all who performed "honest toil." The editor of Philadelphia's *Mechanics Free Press* presented the case for a broad definition of the term "working man": "If an employer superintends his own business (still working with his own hands) he is a working man. . . . If this view of things be correct, shall we look with a jealous eye on those employers who prefer being considered working men? Who are willing to join us in obtaining our objects?" In practice only lawyers, bankers, and brokers were excluded from the fellowship. Indeed, many of the movement's leaders would have been hard pressed to recall the last time they had labored with their "own hands." Several of them were radical reformers who were attracted to the workingmen's movement because, as historian Edward Pessen states, they "held that the greatest crime in society was the denial to the actual producers of wealth [the workers] of the good things they had created."

The injustice against which the workingmen protested in the newspapers, pamphlets, and speeches went far beyond the bread-and-butter issues of long hours and low wages to include such things as imprisonment for debt, religious establishment, unfair taxation, corporate charters that granted to favored individuals virtual monopolies in banking and commerce, an unjust militia system, and poor housing. However, what makes the movement so significant to the student of educational history is the fact that, during its lively if brief history, the inequity against which the leaders of the workingmen's parties rallied most vigorously was that of limited educational opportunity. To their way of thinking no greater obstacle stood in

the way of the attainment of personal status and the achievement of a truly just society. Descriptions of the potential powers of schooling by such men as Jefferson and Franklin had
not fallen on deaf ears. The philosophies and experiments in
educational reform of Pestalozzi and Fellenberg were enthusi-
astically detailed in the workingmen's press. Education would
provide children with the means of realizing economic success.
Education would inform the rising generation of its rights and
privileges, thus arming them against the schemes of conniving
politicians and monopolists. A new generation trained in common schools would surely undo the wrongs of society and
finally achieve the social goals of the American Revolution. For
Robert Dale Owen, late of New Harmony and now a leader in
the New York City Working Mans Party, education was "the
Shibboleth of our cause. We cannot have a better Shibboleth.
It is the chief—we had almost said the only—essential of our
political creed."

From the pens of the leaders of the workingmen's parties
came one of the earliest expressions of American faith in education as a panacea. These spokesmen might have differed to
some extent in their conceptions of the first or primary goal of
public education, but they were unanimous in their conviction
that the schools could achieve wonders. Thus Frances Wright,
one of the leading radical reformers of the day, wrote of the
common school's crucial role in the attainment of a democratic
society: "Until equality be planted in the mind, in the habits,
in the manners, in the feelings, think not it can ever be in the
condition." Stephen Simpson of Philadelphia described knowledge as "the great remedy for intemperance: for in proportion
as we elevate men in the scale of existence . . . so do we reclaim
them from all temptation of degrading vice and ruinous crimes.
A reading and intellectual people were never known to be sot-
tish. . . . Thus sobriety and political honesty are the twin off-
springs of education." George Henry Evans, editor of New
York's *Working Man's Advocate*, was convinced that education
"would remove the veil of ignorance by which the poor who

suffer are prevented from penetrating the mysteries of that legislation of the rich by which their sufferings are produced."

Yet, what future did schooling as it was currently constituted provide for the children of the workers? In most parts of the nation, as we have seen, public funds for education were limited to the support of pauper schooling. Quality education was private, costly, and thus, for most children, inaccessible. In its financial grants to private academies and colleges the states were, in effect, supporting a system that granted the wealthier classes a virtual monopoly on secondary and higher education. Therefore, in a program calling for broad economic and social reform, the workingmen's parties gave educational reform top priority. Philadelphia's *Mechanic's Free Press* placed the demand for a free, tax-supported school system on its masthead. In New York City the masthead of the *Working Man's Advocate* read, "All children are entitled to equal education; all adults to equal privileges." A report of a committee of the Philadelphia workingmen's party in 1830, not willing to restrict its call to elementary schooling, demanded as well a system of higher education that would break "the present monopoly of talent." The previous year the Philadelphia party, in polling candidates it considered supporting, had asked as its first question whether the office seeker deemed it essential for future generations "that an open school and competent teachers for every child from the lowest branch of an infant school to the lecture rooms of practical science should be established and those who supervise them should be chosen by the people."

While party spokesmen in Philadelphia and New York took the lead and were most vocal in their demands for educational reform, the cause was by no means restricted to these cities. *The Working Man's Advocate* of April 17, 1830 reported that the Farmers' and Mechanics' Association of Lyme, Connecticut had resolved to condemn the legislature for its financial aid to colleges and churches, implying that neither of these institutions benefited the educational needs of the masses of people. In Massachusetts the New England Association of Farmers,

Mechanics and Other Working Men, a confederation of work-ingmen's parties formed in 1831, established a committee on education. This group not only worked to further the cause of public education but revealed the shocking conditions of child labor in the cotton mills. Among other things, the committee reported that mill children, working in excess of 13½ hours a day, had no opportunity for education other than on Sundays or after 8 P.M. during the six-day work week. If parents desired to remove their children from work for short periods in order that they receive a modicum of schooling, certain loss of employment followed.

Records of the workingmen's organizations attest to more than just demands for reform in terms of control and availability of schooling. There was also deep concern over the quality of the curriculum, teaching methods, and physical facilities. Party spokesmen found the existing public and charity schools overcrowded, the discipline overly strict, and the curricula and teaching methods sterile and unimaginative. They encouraged "instruction in the laws of our country" and student discussion of political questions. They deprecated the overemphasis upon memorization. While acknowledging the ineffectiveness of all too many teachers, they were among the first to attribute much of the blame for this to inadequate regard for professional training and to the meager salaries teachers received for their efforts. George Henry Evans of *The Working Man's Advocate* asked, "Are teachers estimated in proportion to their skill and experience, or to their servility to the Trustees?" In another issue of his paper he compared the rewards of the teachers who labored "early and late, six days out of seven, for *two* or *three* hundred dollars a year" with that of the preachers who rarely "get less than *five hundred*, and few less than *a thousand* dollars a year, for laboring one, two, or three days out of seven." Continuing, Evans asked, "Does the TEACHER of things necessary to be done and avoided *here*, get as well compensated for the six days' labor which he is required to perform each week, as the PREACHER about *hereafter* does for the one day's labor required of *him*?"

Evans' gibe at the clergy, like the voiced opposition of the workingmen of Lyme to state support of churches, is indicative of a general hostility on the part of labor leaders to religious influence in political and educational affairs. Also identified as enemies of the cause were the captains of industry and commerce. A typical expression of this attitude was aired by Stephen Simpson, who insisted that "the effort of capital and power, is always on the side of ignorance in the people." The rich and powerful, he declared, feared losing "exclusive privileges by imparting knowledge to the mass of the people."

By 1831 the artisans' ventures into organized, crusading party politics were coming to an end. The life of the workingmen's parties essentially coincided with an economic depression which struck the nation during the years 1828–1831. The improbability of waging successful strikes during a period of business decline and a general hostility toward union activities by the courts were quite apparently crucial in the decision to turn to politics. But the parties proved unsuccessful. They had failed to achieve the primary goal of all such organizations: to win elections. Behind this failure were a number of contributing factors: inadequate funds, inexperienced leadership, and self-seeking opportunists among the membership. Also, on occasion, basic philosophical differences between the more radical-utopian fringe of the parties and the rank-and-file craftsmen led to intraparty squabbles. To cite one example, in New York City a serious party schism arose over Robert Dale Owen's proposal to foster democratic education through the establishment of public boarding schools whose curricula and teaching methods would be modeled after those of Pestalozzi and Fellenberg. While a number of labor journals and party leaders supported the idea, from all appearances what the majority of the members wished for their children was access to noncharity, traditional elementary schooling.

With the demise of the parties the artisans once again turned to more traditional tactics and more traditional objectives. The year 1833 witnessed the establishment of trades' unions in New York City, Baltimore, Philadelphia, and Washington, D.C.

By 1836 similar organizations had been founded in Newark, New Brunswick, Albany, Troy, Schenectady, Boston, Pittsburgh, Cincinnati, and Louisville. The spectacular rise of the trades' union movement was due to far more than a recognition that the era of the workingmen's parties was over. The fact was that an upswinging economy only intensified the conditions against which the workers had initially organized to protest: further decline in the status of the journeymen and the apprentice system, increased reliance on female, child, and immigrant labor, longer hours, and lower wages. The attainment of decent salaries and working conditions became the crucial and immediate objectives with the strike the most potent weapon. Education did not disappear from the speeches and writings of labor leaders. Instead, its position in the hierarchy of goals was shifted. Whereas it once stood as the primary means by which the good life was to be attained, as the chief weapon for revealing and defeating labor's enemies, education was now depicted as a much-desired fruit to be gained through the victory of other causes. For example, in Boston labor's *cause célèbre* in 1835 was the 10-hour working day. Theophilus Fiske, however, urged the unionists to insist instead on an 8-hour maximum. "... eight hours for work, eight hours for sleep, eight hours for amusement and instruction" he deemed "the equitable allotment of the twenty-four."

The workingmen's movement of skilled craftsmen, dedicated leaders, and assorted dreamers could not survive the Panic of 1837. While it succeeded in achieving few of its goals, idealistic or pragmatic, from the vantage point that history provides it cannot be written off as a total failure. Edward Pessen writes, "If it is the function of radical parties in America to act as gadflies, to goad and influence, rather than win elections, then the Working Men succeeded admirably." It was precisely as "gadflies" that the parties and the trades' unions contributed to the cause of common schooling. In providing a home base for reformers, they put at their disposal a platform from which to declare their immense faith in the power of learning and their warning that, without a system of free, universal, and public schooling, social democracy could not be achieved. The labor leaders in fact constituted the first major wave of the education reform movement that was to commence in full force at almost the exact moment the strength of the trades' unions waned. Their insistence that labor was the creator of all wealth and their desire to see the emergence of a fundamentally socialistic society identifies them as radical reformers as opposed to the solid moderates who later assumed leadership of the common-school movement. As Pessen points out, if they had devoted their efforts to articulating a scheme of social revolution, it is likely that their influence would have been nil. For clearly, not even the status-conscious artisans, whose cause they espoused, would have been responsive. It is quite possible that they hoped that educational reform would result in a new generation dedicated to wide-ranging social change, but in their public pronouncements they described the benefits of universal public schooling in terms that, with a few exceptions, were attractive to men of more conservative temperament. When labor leaders spoke of education as a means to "elevate the moral and intellectual powers," to "spread sobriety and virtue," and to eliminate the need for "jails and state prisons, penitentiaries and almshouses, houses of correction and popular executions," affirmative nods could not be denied even by those to whom the very existence of a workingmen's movement was cause for alarm.

The Democratic Party in the northeastern states had been most affected by the challenge of the workingmen's parties. Not only did the two compete for the support of labor, but they both laid claim to the banner of Jacksonian democracy. Sensing the threat, the Democrats were quick to adopt planks from the workingmen's platforms when it seemed expedient. This was certainly true of educational reform, when the Democrats in the middle 1830s subscribed to what historian Rush Welter terms "anarchy with a schoolmaster." They called for state governments that would restore equality of opportunity through a policy of economic liberalism coupled with the extension and improvement of public education. Let the legislatures, they urged, serve all the people by ceasing to foster monopoly through charters and grants to canal companies, special acts of incorporation to favored banks and support of private academies and colleges. With special interests curbed and the miraculous powers of schooling made available to all, the pie of prosperity would once more be within reach of the general populace. Throughout the 1830s and 1840s this economic and education package was espoused by leading Democrats, among them Governors Wolf of Pennsylvania, Marcy of New York, and Morton of Massachusetts. Joining with them were major party organs, including the New York *Evening Post*, edited by William Cullen Bryant, Walt Whitman's Brooklyn *Daily Eagle*, and the *United States Magazine and Democratic Review*.

The leadership of the Democratic Party was able to achieve a small measure of success for its school program. In New York and Massachusetts more money for the common schools was made available under Democratic administrations. In Pennsylvania Governor Wolf successfully led the fight for the state's first meaningful school law, passed in 1834. However, the very nature of the party's membership and the core of its philosophy militated against its initiating truly effective common-school reform. In these three states the party depended heavily on the support of the farmers, and this, with the exception of the Scotch Irish of Western Pennsylvania, was precisely the segment of the population most hostile to increased taxation for education. In Pennsylvania Democrats among the various German pietistic sects were particularly opposed to public education, which they envisioned as a threat to their own system of schools. So it was that in this state Democrats were among the most vigorous opponents of the school law of 1834, while a Whig, Thaddeus Stevens, issued the most eloquent appeal against its repeal. Throughout the nation the party's commitment to democracy and *laissez-faire* engendered a fervent espousal of the cause of local control of education at a time when the great need was for more leader- ship, supervision, and coordination on the state level.

Thus, although the Democratic Party in the North was the first of the major parties to strongly advocate the principle of democratic education, it cannot be credited with initiating the larger share of school-reform legislation. Ironically, the cause of public education, which had, in large measure, been launched politically by the workingmen and adopted by the Democrats, was dominated during the late 1830s and 1840s by men asso- ciated with the Whig Party. It would perhaps be appropriate at this point to recall Emerson's observation that the Democrats had the best principles, the Whigs the best men. However, there were more complex causes for the course of events.

The Whig Party had originally been formed by a union of diverse interests united only by a hatred of what they termed "Jacksonian mobocracy" and a desire for political power. En- compassed by this party, this what has been called "organized incompatibility," were Southern planters demanding free trade and claiming the right of nullification as well as Northern mer- chants and Western agriculturists who supported Clay's "Amer- ican System" of protective tariffs and internal improvements. In the Northeast the party drew its support largely from middle-class farmers, merchants, professional people, and in- tellectuals who contemplated with optimism the possibilities of economic nationalism and at the same time shuddered with anxiety at the dislocations they saw arising in society. The most thoughtful among them were by no means antidemocratic, but they were concerned that an uneducated electorate might de- stroy the fabric of the American political system. Tocqueville echoed the fears of many when he wrote:

If ever the free institutions of America are destroyed, that event may be attributed to the unlimited authority of the ma- jority, which may at some future time urge the minority to desperation, and oblige them to have recourse to physical force.

Anarchy will then be the result, but it will have been brought about by despotism.

The concerns of many of the solid middle class were not stirred exclusively from below. They were also fostered by the excesses of power and wealth that were being concentrated in the hands of that small group of industrial capitalists emerging with the growth of the factory system. Associating this danger with the need to expand educational opportunity, Horace Mann wrote, "If one class possesses all the wealth and education, while the residue of society is ignorant and poor, it matters not by what name the relation between them may be called: the latter, in fact and in truth, will be the servile dependents and subjects of the former." Surely an industrial feudalism was no more attractive than the anarchy of the mob.

What the "good folk" sought to preserve and extend was a society of order and opportunity, a system that rewarded righteous behavior and honest toil with material comfort and the responsibilities of leadership. This was the "American Way" they depicted as being inherited from the Founding Fathers and refined during the early national period. It was a structure dependent not only on the maintenance of republican institutions but also on the existence of a climate of Christian morality. During a period when, to most, religion and morality were synonymous, a number of developments did not seem to bode well for society. Separation of church and state had lessened the influence of the clergy in secular matters. The schismatic tendencies of Protestant sects prevented a unified defense against the growing strength of the Catholic Church. And it seemed quite possible that in the emerging city slums and out in the frontier wilderness religion might be shut out entirely.

The Whigs in the Northeast and West responded to the pleas of educational reformers because the common school was presented to them as the best hope for their "American Way." So many of the reform leaders themselves had risen from humble beginnings to positions of stature. They were men concerned over the threats of injustice, inequality, and immorality, yet, at the same time, they were terribly optimistic that their brand of reform, almost by itself, could right society's ills. They were as one with the political Whigs in their faith in the state government as a positive force in social as well as economic endeavors. They shared an allegiance to Protestant-based cultural homogeneity. Unlike the radicals among the workingmen's parties, they had no desire to reconstruct the system. Unlike the Democrats, they felt no keen distrust of centralized government. America, they believed, was essentially sound. Growths that threatened the body politic could be removed through the miraculous curative power of universal common schooling. With this accomplished the evolutionary process of national development could continue on its way. By the middle 1830s the common-school movement was firmly under the guidance of those who would see it through to final victory. These were good, solid, moderate men, totally committed to a society of morality and equal opportunity and totally convinced that their cause held the key to attaining it.

Unlike many significant events in history, it is impossible to assign a date on which the common-school movement took on the dimensions of a crusade. But certainly June 30, 1837 was of signal importance because it marked the beginning of Horace Mann's career as Secretary of the Massachusetts State Board of Education. The establishment of the Board earlier that year had resulted, in large measure, from the efforts of the pioneer reformer James Carter and the new Whig governor Edward Everett. To both men an essential step in removing the public schools of Massachusetts from the doldrums of district management was the assumption by the state of a direct role in their supervision. No great power was granted to the Board by the legislature. It was required to collect and disseminate information regarding the state's schools and report annually to the legislature on the general condition of education in the Commonwealth. As its paid secretary, Mann was expected to do the Board's leg work, to travel from town to town, gather information, propagandize for improved schools, and prepare annual reports.

From this very modest power base Mann proceeded not only to direct the reform of the educational system of Massachusetts but also to become the foremost leader of the common-school movement in the nation. He was the epitome of the dedicated Yankee reformer of the era, completely convinced of the righteousness of his cause, and willing to spare no effort to attain his goals. He entered upon his new task with gusto, writing on July 2, 1837, "My lawbooks are for sale. My office is to let! The bar is no longer my forum. My jurisdiction is changed. I have abandoned jurisprudence, and betaken myself to the larger sphere of mind and morals." The urgent pace never slackened during the years he served the Board. Traveling throughout the state he encouraged school committees and citizens to commit themselves to greater efforts on behalf of their children's education. He assembled teachers at institutes and conventions; he founded and edited the *Common School Journal*; he journeyed all through the nation and abroad; he corresponded with educational leaders in nearly every state. All this to promote the cause in its several ramifications. Not only did he see fit to present arguments in behalf of the principle of common schooling, but he was also very much concerned with the total effectiveness of the educational process. His reports, speeches, and editorials ranged widely to include discussions of educational organization and administration, school architecture, teacher training, curriculum reform, salaries, tenure, methodology, and a host of other matters. Mann's own words provide a clue to the intensity of his efforts: "From the time I accepted the secretaryship... until May 1848, when I tendered my resignation, I never took a single day for recreation, and months and months together passed without my withdrawing a single evening to call on a friend."

What kind of man was this who at 41 gave up a lucrative law practice and the presidency of the state senate to embark on a crusade that might well have led to anonymity? The answer to this question reveals not only the character of Horace Mann but also clues to understanding the driving forces behind that whole group of men and women who passionately believed in and fought for the several social causes in an age of panaceas. A great many of these people shared similar backgrounds with Mann. Indeed, the number throughout the country who had been raised in New England and/or, like Mann, received a Calvinist upbringing is truly remarkable.

Mann's youth was filled with the kinds of experiences that one might imagine are conducive to shaping a dedicated reformer. Fatherless from the age of 13, he assumed more than a boy's share of the toil required to scratch a living from the rocky soil of Franklin, Massachusetts. He obviously found scant comfort in the Calvinist preachings of his minister, the Rev. Nathaniel Emmons, who favored vivid descriptions of sinful man, a harsh God, and the fires of Hell. We know from Mann's recollections that these sermons brought him many nights of fitful dreams. In later years he abandoned the Calvinism of his childhood to embrace the more humane tenets of Unitarianism, but he never shook off the Puritan emphasis on the necessity for society to be governed by a strict moral code. The Unitarian in him that expressed itself in a deep faith in the essential goodness of man and the nearly limitless potential of human institutions always existed alongside an abiding Puritanism that led him, on various occasions, to angrily condemn such "vices" as profanity, drinking, smoking, and ballet dancing.

Like his religious experience Mann's personal school career was marked by contrasting shades of light and dark. Up to the age of 16 he attended the town school, but he was never able to be present for more than 8 to 10 weeks in any given year. And that institution offered a microcosm of the conditions in the schools of Massachusetts that Mann would later strive to correct. The curriculum was narrow, the teaching methods stultifying, and the teachers as cruel as they were ignorant. Yet the New England traditions of hard work and commitment to learning were evident in the Mann family, and he was encouraged to further his education. At 20 he began a six-month period of intensive study under the tutelage of an itinerant teacher named Barrett. This was sufficient to earn him entry to Brown University with sophomore standing. It was of no little significance that Mann achieved his first real success in life through an educational endeavor, assisted by an able, inspiring teacher.

Mann's political and social outlook was first revealed in his student essays at Brown. They evidence a strong regional pride coupled with attachment to the Union. There are affirmations of support for such liberal principles as freedom of the press, separation of church and state, and unrestricted immigration. He expressed a deep concern for the problems that beset society, but he also displayed an optimistic faith in the power of human compassion and free, republican institutions to remedy all wrongs. Even at this early stage in his life Mann declared his belief that popular education was the most crucial element in achieving social well-being.

In 1819, after delivering his commencement oration on "The Progressive Character of the Human Race," Mann received his degree with high honors. In 1823 he began his law career in Dedham, Massachusetts. The intervening years had been spent as a Latin tutor at his alma mater and as a student at the famous law school at Litchfield, Connecticut. He was elected to the lower house of the Massachusetts legislature in 1827 as a National Republican (later Whig). After six years in the lower chamber he successfully ran for the state Senate, where he remained until called to the Board of Education. Mann was not only a member of the legislature that passed the bill establishing the Board but as president of the Senate his signature was affixed to it.

During his legislative career Mann had displayed the characteristics of a Whiggish reformer. Lawrence Cremin explains that Mann chose to run as a National Republican because "his temper was far too conservatively moralistic to cater to the crowd." His concerns were with political and economic as well as social morality, and on this ground he looked askance at what he considered an onslaught by the Jacksonian "mob" on orderly rule, property rights, and judicial supremacy. The humanitarian reformers of Mann's persuasion were determined to uphold and strengthen the system, not overturn it. They believed that weaknesses could be remedied and injustices eliminated without resorting to radical nostrums. In the humane society that they envisioned, business would philanthropically employ a share of its profits to benefit the people as a whole. Thus Mann was not the least bit inconsistent when, after a dramatic maiden speech in the legislature defending religious liberty, his next address was devoted to a highly optimistic portrait of the great advantages which would accrue from the expansion of the railroads.

Throughout his career in the state legislature Mann's efforts were directed toward broad reform. He led the struggle for better care of the mentally ill that resulted in an act establishing the nation's first state hospital for the insane at Worcester. Moral principles coupled with sympathy for the poor encouraged him to participate in a drive to control the sale of alcoholic beverages. In 1836 his bill making public drinking a crime became law. He joined the Prison Discipline Society and helped propagate their call for prisons for reform as well as punishment. His interests extended to such areas as support of a society for the prevention of pauperism and defense of the right of handicapped Negro children to benefit from the special educational facilities that had been provided exclusively for whites.

Horace Mann, successful lawyer, effective politician, and dedicated reformer, was an obvious candidate for the position of secretary to the Board, and he accepted the $1000-a-year job with enthusiasm. He had never been happy in legal practice, and the secretaryship offered a potentially far wider audience for his reform appeals than did the halls of the legislature.

Also, it is quite likely that by 1837 he had already come to the conclusion that the common school had the potential to be, as he later described it, the "centre and circumference" of the "wheel of Progress":

If I can be the means of ascertaining what is the best construction of [school] houses, what are the best books, what is the best mode of instruction; if I can discover by what appliance of means a non-thinking, non-reflecting, non-speaking child can most surely be trained into a noble citizen, ready to contend for the right, *and to die for the* right; *if I can only obtain and diffuse throughout the state a few good ideas on these and similar subjects, may I not flatter myself that my ministry has not been wholly in vain?*

Before discussing the ideas and arguments that led Mann to achieve the position of foremost spokesman for public education, it is essential to call attention to the fact that, during the same year he accepted the secretaryship, he embraced the doctrines of phrenology. Phrenology may be discarded today as "stuff and nonsense," but as a forerunner to modern psychology it did offer some valid conclusions, although they were based largely on incorrect assumptions. The phrenologists insisted that each mental factor was governed by an organ of the brain. These organs controlled a total of 43 faculties, generally grouped under nine major categories: animal, domestic, moral, self-perfecting, sensory, perceptive, literary, reflecting, and aspiring. Contrary to commonly accepted belief of the day, the phrenologists taught that there were natural differences among men in their mental and moral propensities due to variances from one person to another in the vigor of the several organs. The bumps and crannies of the head, they believed, could reveal to a skilled examiner the relative influence (vigor) on an individual of each of the faculties. Thus a phrenologist who had examined Mann's head declared, "We seldom find so large a brain in the tophead, in the region of

the organs of reason, imagination, sympathy, dignity, persever-
ance, wit, and moral sentiment, joined with so little basilar
brain in the animal and selfish organ."

Mann's attachment to phrenology was so strong that he was
ready to recommend its study to teachers and to refer to its
findings time and again in his lectures. He once stated that a
young man would be wise to spend his last dollar in learning
from a phrenological examination what his career should be.
Mann shared, with intellectuals of his day, a fascination for
what appeared to be scientific explanations of natural phenomena, and this probably explains a large part of his initial
attraction to phrenology. But he obviously also found phrenology's strong advocacy of education with particular stress on
the laws of health and moral training quite appealing. Though
its views on individual differences had shaken Mann's earlier
belief that "there is by nature little, or perhaps no distinctions
among men with respect to their original powers of intellect,"
he gained great satisfaction from the "science's" creed that a
proper curriculum, effectively taught, could encourage the
fullest development of the positive propensities while checking
those that were socially harmful. With its optimistic faith in
the powers of education to better mankind, phrenology added
support to Mann's reform impulse and affected his thinking in
the areas of curriculum and methodology.

For Horace Mann the mission of the common school was to
be nothing less than to provide opportunities for the fullest
development of each individual, to guarantee progress through
social harmony, and to ensure that the republic would be
guided by an intelligent, moral citizenry. He was not original
or unique in his advocacy of such goals, but no predecessor
or contemporary had presented them so convincingly, enunci-
ated so effectively their importance, or described in such detail
how they could best be attained. From the beginning Mann was
insistent that the public schools must not only provide quality
education but must also be truly common. The greatest
need, as Mann envisioned it, was to offset the potential threats
to social unity inherent in several trends of the time: the wid-

ening gap between rich and poor, the schismatic tendencies in religion, the growing heterogeneity of the population, and political and sectional divisiveness. Mann was certain the schools would accomplish wonders if they could first gather under their roofs the children of all the people:

It is on this common platform, that a general acquaintanceship should be formed between the children of the same neighborhood. It is here, that the affinities of a common nature should unite them together so as to give the advantages of preoccupancy and a stable possession of fraternal feelings, against the alienating competitions of subsequent life.

Bringing the children together was only the initial step. The most important task was to provide them with the kinds of experiences most likely to achieve the school's educational objectives. For Mann these included the sharing of a common intellectual experience, preparation for the duties of citizenship, and, above all, the inculcation of a common code of Christian morality. Moral education was at the very heart of Mann's conception of the common school—a first cause. He viewed it as "a primal necessity of social existence." Phrenology had taught him that the "unrestrained passions of men are not only homicidal, but suicidal; and a community without a conscience would soon extinguish itself." The need for this kind of training, he insisted, was immediate, because "As the relations of men become more complex, and the business of the world more extended, new opportunities and new temptations for wrong-doing have been created." Mann inherited from his Puritan forebears the ability to awesomely portray examples of immorality. However, he had a more attractive alternative than Calvinist hellfire to offer his audience:

. . . to all doubters, disbelievers, or despairers, in human progress, it may still be said, there is one experiment which has never yet been tried. It is an experiment which, even before its

inception, offers the highest authority for its ultimate success. Its formula is intelligible to all. . . . It is expressed in these few and simple words: "Train up a child in the way he should go, and when he is old he will not depart from it."

The argument for moral education was typical of the approach Mann employed as he strove for support of the common school. First his readers and listeners were made well aware of the existence and danger to society of vice, ignorance, and poverty. Then they were assured of the curative powers of education. There is naught but "woe to the republic that rests upon no better foundation than ignorance, selfishness, and passion." But a republic, whose citizens are virtuous and enlightened as to the "great essentials of political knowledge" and to their rights and responsibilities, will surely flourish.

In attempting to promote the cause of tax-supported education, Mann recognized that it was crucial to win over the propertied class. His fifth, tenth, and twelfth reports contained brilliant appeals to their self-interest, sense of civic responsibility, and fears. Here was the phrenologist-teacher fully aware of the propensities for good and evil in man. In the *Fifth Annual Report* (1841) Mann reminded his readers of the money value of an educated worker. Then, playing on their anxieties, he asked:

. . . could there, in your opinion, be any police so vigilant and effective, for the protection of all the rights of person, property, and character, as such a sound and comprehensive education and training, as our system of Common Schools could be made to impart: and would not the payment of a sufficient tax to make such educational training universal, be the cheapest means of self-protection and insurance?

In the *Tenth Annual Report* (1846) Mann argued that education was a natural right to which the property of the commonwealth is pledged for support. The *Twelfth Annual Report*

(1848) contains Mann's most urgent appeals to the middle class, his own class. In it he called to mind the growing chasm being created between "overgrown wealth and desperate poverty" and the danger of "feudalism" on the one hand and "agrarianism" (socialism) on the other. But, once more the answer:

Education beyond all other devices of human origin, is the greater equalizer of the conditions of men—the balance-wheel of the social machinery. . . . It does better than to disarm the poor of their hostility towards the rich; it prevents being poor. . . . The spread of education, by enlarging the cultivated class or caste, will open a wider area over which the social feelings will expand; and, if this education should be universal and complete, it would do more than all things to obliterate factitious distinctions in society.

The twelfth report was prepared after Mann had made his decision to retire from the Board of Education. As Curti points out, this fact, joined with a series of rather frustrating attempts to gain the support of mill barons, probably accounts for his inclusion of rather strongly worded warnings of the dangers inherent in a selfish industrial-capitalist class. Such statements were untypical of Mann, who was not one to bite the hand that might feed education. Never hesitant to describe the ills of society, he generally avoided blame seeking, choosing instead to speak of the remedial powers of schooling. What Mann sincerely desired, and what he felt the common school could uniquely achieve, was social harmony. Religion and the Bible would be very much present in the classroom but offered in such a manner as to emphasize principles and beliefs common to all Protestants regardless of sectarian differences. Mann placed great import on citizenship training, but, once again, the stress was to be on unity. The children were to be made aware of the workings of government and of the duties and rights they all would share as citizens, "those articles in the creed of republicanism, which are accepted by all, believed in by all, and which form the common basis of our political faith." However, under no circumstance was a school class to focus on issues which align group against group, party against party:

... *when the teacher, in the course of his lesson or lecture on the fundamental law, arrives at a controversial text, he is either to read it without comment or remark; or, at most, he is only to say that the passage is the subject of disputation, and that the schoolroom is neither the tribunal to adjudicate, nor the forum to discuss it.*

It is quite obvious that Mann's formula for political training was self-defeating. To ingest laws and rules while virtually ignoring the great issues can neither inspire interest nor lead to a real understanding of the functions of government. Also, as shall be discussed later in detail, Mann's approach to religious education left much to be desired, particularly in the eyes of Catholics and conservative Protestants. Yet, as their acceptance by reformers throughout the country attests, these proposals were strategically sound. How else could one achieve support for a common school from a population barely convinced that sufficient commonality existed to constitute a nation, varying in its allegiance to democratic principles, and uncertain of the wisdom of removing education from the domain of the church?

Mann's influence on educational reform went well beyond the realm of thought regarding the value and purposes to be served by the common school. There was hardly a subject of concern to education on which he did not speak out, and few of his ideas failed to gain acceptance as gospel by his counterparts throughout the nation. He favored the traditional curriculum of the three Rs, English grammar, and geography, offering little encouragement to the manual training idea in vogue among some educationists:

The development of the common nature; the cultivation of the germs of intelligence, uprightness, benevolence, truth, that belongs to all: these are the principal, the aim, the end—while special preparations for the field or the shop, for the forum, or the desk, for the land or the sea, are but incident.

There were, however, two novel subjects Mann wished added to the standard offerings: physiology and vocal music. Both were valued by the adherents of phrenology as contributors to intellectual and moral development. It should be understood that Mann was not suggesting the introduction of subjects on the grounds of aesthetic merit. Music was proposed primarily for its mathematical challenge and its supposed ability to calm the savage breast of child and man.

It was in the area of the teaching-learning process that Mann was most innovative. Committed to a common curriculum, yet convinced that individuals differed in their intellectual and moral capacities, he placed great faith in the power of competent teachers employing modern methods to ensure the fullest development of each child. Mann was an enthusiast for Pestalozzian principles, a position strengthened by his trip to Europe in 1843. He urged abandonment of harsh discipline and endless drills. These, he insisted, in the long run led children to either utterly reject the precepts they were forced to memorize or to obey them with blind acceptance. Neither outcome was desirable in a morally ordered, republican society. He asked teachers not to impose learning but to strive to instruct in such a way that children would appreciate and understand what they were being taught. This could best be accomplished by treating each child as an individual, by stressing rewards rather than punishment, by appealing through affection rather than fear, and by utilizing more of the inductive techniques and less rote learning. Along with able teachers and progressive methods, Mann also desired to secure an improved physical environment for education. Both the principles of phrenology and sense realism stressed that pleasant, well equipped surroundings were highly conducive to learning. To Mann the dilapidated, unsanitary public schools all too familiar throughout the state were an abomination.

Mann labored for 12 years to obtain the common schools he envisioned. He asked parents who supported private schools to believe enough in the common-school ideal to enroll their children. He prodded school boards and the state legislature to provide increased funds for books, equipment, school buildings, salaries, and teacher-training facilities. He lectured teachers on the merits of the new European techniques and the propriety of a more humane attitude toward children. His efforts were directed primarily toward improvements in his own state, but, because of the forceful eloquence with which he expressed his views and because he was the major educational figure in a state that had always led in public schooling, reformers throughout the land looked to him as their leader and example. Henry Barnard, who directed school reform in Rhode Island and Connecticut and who was second only to Mann in national prominence, wrote these words to his Massachusetts colleague: "You are my guide, my hope, my friend, my fellow-laborer and fellow-sufferer in 'the cause.'"

Caution must be exercised before declaring any individual to be a paradigm or the typical model of a modern major general. Mann certainly held points of view and opinions that were not shared or not shared as passionately by other school reformers. In comparing the outlooks of Mann and Barnard, Merle Curti calls attention to a number of instances in which the latter took more conservative positions. Barnard was not totally opposed to a moderate use of drill in the classroom; "his conception of character formation was more definitely orthodox and more specifically religious" than Mann's; he was less inclined to look askance at the excesses of industrial capitalism, and, unlike Mann, he advocated the inclusion of history in the classroom as stimulant to patriotism, despite its glorification of war. However, when it came to defining the basic principles and articles of faith of the common-school movement, Mann was unquestionably the chief spokesman. Whether one turns to Samuel Lewis in Ohio, to Ninian Edwards in Illinois, to Calvin Wiley in North Carolina, or to Robert Breckinridge in Kentucky, all spokesmen for school reform, one finds reiterated Mann's blend of conservative support of the establishment, awareness of and concern for the sufferings and injustices that threatened social stability, and unbending faith in the power of common schooling to cure the ills and perpetuate the good. One finds repeated Mann's determination to promote social harmony by gathering together children from all walks of life and, in common, carefully nurturing their moral and intellectual development. Among most of the leaders there was also a general acceptance of the new teaching methods and an appreciation of the need to provide professional training for teachers. And they all shared with Horace Mann a wearisome struggle to overcome the apathy and prejudices of their constituents. These men endure as heroes of public education not only for the ideas they articulated but also for the battles they fought and won.

chapter three

issues of controversy, fruits of victory

the proponents of the common school were forced to contend with numerous obstacles on the road to reform. Some were overcome in a relatively calm atmosphere through persistent employment of rational arguments. But many individuals, parties, and interest groups regarded various aspects of the common-school ideal as threatening. When the plans of reformers clashed with religious beliefs, regional prejudices, long-established teaching practices, and political philosophies, the air became charged and the controversy bitter. The case studies in conflict that follow are presented not only to portray the course of significant events during the era of the common school but also to identify and illustrate the roots of issues and controversies that have marked the development of education to this day. For, the success of the reformers, while grand, was by no means complete. What they achieved was a *beginning* of the common school, largely through an effective, but by no means total, checking of the opposition.

The reformers' desire to establish a nonsectarian religious atmosphere in the schools appears to the modern reader to be far from a radical proposal. Indeed, in view of the neglect of the sensitivities of atheists, Catholics, and Jews, it would, by today's standards, be judged downright illiberal. Mann's position on excluding sectarian influences seems eminently logical. As he put it, "if a government would recognize and protect the rights of religious freedom, it must abstain from subjecting the capacities of its children to any legal standard of religious faith, with as great fidelity as it abstains from controlling the opinions of men." His insistence that the common schools were in fact Christian in character appears incontestable:

I have felt bound to show, that, so far from its being an irreligious, an anti-Christian, or an un-Christian system, it is a system which recognizes religious obligations in their fullest extent; that it is a system which invokes a religious spirit, and can never be fully administered without such a spirit; that it inculcates the great commands, upon which hang all the law and the prophets; that it welcomes the Bible, and therefore welcomes all the doctrines which the Bible really contains, and that it listens to these doctrines so reverently, that, for the time being, it will not suffer any rash mortal to thrust in interpolations of their meaning, or overlay the text with any of the "many inventions" which the heart of man has sought out. It is a system, however, which leaves open all other means of instruction,—the pulpits, the Sunday schools, the Bible classes, the catechisms, of all denominations,—to be employed according to the preferences of individual parents.

Yet a number of conservative clergymen were violently opposed to Mann's point of view. They considered all this to be part of the movement to completely sever ties that had existed between church and commonwealth since Puritan days. In the Western world religions had traditionally been the primary sponsors and supporters of education, and schooling, particularly elementary schooling, had always had as its first objective the inculcation of the doctrines of faith. Even the establishment of public schools in colonial New England had not represented a serious departure from historical precedent. Given the religious character of the curriculum and the prescribed role of ministers in their governance, the seventeenth-century schools might best be described as public-parochial institutions. Not only did Mann's brand of nonsectarian religion appear contrary to these traditions, to many it also smacked mightily of an attempt to impose a Unitarian outlook on the schools. His apparent rejection of the concept of man's innate depravity and advocacy of more humane approaches to teaching were pointed to as further evidence of such a plot. Had not the leading Unitarian minister, William Ellery Channing, as early as 1833 in his "Remarks on Education," urged that teaching be founded on love, and that teachers recognize the interests, needs, and potential of their children and avoid the deadening routine of enforced memorization of meaningless information?

The first major confrontation arose in 1838. That year, in hope of stimulating local school committees to expand their schools' libraries, Mann arranged with a publisher to produce two series of books, one designed for younger children and one for more advanced students. The publishers were instructed to obtain authors representing varying political and religious persuasions and to ensure that no volume contained material that could be considered of a doctrinal nature. No work in the series would be accepted without prior approval of every member of the state Board. Mann was determined that the series not be offensive to any group. In this he was not only following the dictates of his own philosophy but also adhering to the letter of the law of 1827, which specifically stated that school committees "shall never direct any school book to be purchased or used, in any of the schools under their superintendence, which are calculated to favor any particular religious sect or tenet."

Controversy arose when a book of quite definite sectarian leanings was offered for the Board's consideration. This was Abbot's *The Child at Home*, a volume in a series published by the American Sunday School Union. The Union's secretary,

Frederick A. Packard, had written to Mann urging its adoption and had received a negative reply on the grounds that the book was clearly doctrinaire and thus had no place in public schools. Packard retaliated in speeches before orthodox Congregationalist clergy in Massachusetts and in letters appearing in a New York newspaper. It did not matter that Packard was a nonresident of Massachusetts and that any other action by Mann and the Board would have been clearly illegal. Many were ready to agree that the Board was following not a nonsectarian but rather a nonreligious policy. The Committee on Education of the Massachusetts House of Representatives echoed this kind of sentiment in a report issued in 1840:

A book upon politics, morals, or religion, containing no party or sectarian views, will be apt to contain no distinct views of any kind, and will be likely to leave the mind in a state of doubt and skepticism, much more to be deplored than any party or sectarian bias.

E. A. Newton, a member of the Board, also took issue with his colleagues' stand and resigned his seat in protest. He was firmly attached to the traditional belief that the school could not fulfill its responsibilities to promote moral values without the aid of sectarian doctrine. In 1844 he once more raised the issue in the columns of the *Christian Witness and Church Advocate*. Mann responded, again insisting that the Christian religion could be and was being taught in the public schools despite the necessary absence of sectarianism.

One of the most colorful and persistent of Mann's adversaries came to the fore in 1846, in the person of the Reverend Matthew Hale Smith. In a sermon entitled "The Ark of God in New Cart" the fiery Calvinist lashed out at the public school reformers with their new methods of discipline and their attempts at nondenominational religious teaching. Regarding their attitude toward holy writ, he declared, "Throwing themselves across the word of God, they practically oppose its lessons. They deny the propriety of an early religious training; they ridicule, as well as forbid, the use of the rod." Smith had no doubts as to who was the chief offender. To Mann he wrote:

1. I regard you as the representative of a system, or its head, which seeks to change, slowly, perhaps, but surely, the whole system of education in the common schools—the result of which will be to elevate the intellectual over the moral, and man above God. In detail and in element I conceive your notions, in this matter, to be crude, their fruits destructive; and the more I see your system explained, the worse, to my mind, it appears.

2. Are you in favor of the use of the rod as the principal means of enforcing obedience? That you tolerate it in deference to public sentiment, I do not dispute. But I am misinformed if you are not against its use, and do not, as you have opportunity, discountenance its use.

In his responses to Smith, to Newton, and to Packard, Mann continuously reiterated his conviction that moral training did take precedence over development of the intellect, that the Bible and general principles of Christianity did belong in the schools. But he remained adamantly opposed to suggestions put forth that sectarian teachings in the schools be made a matter of local option. This, he believed, would only lead to divisiveness and conflict:

Majorities will change in the same place. One sect may have ascendency, today; another, tomorrow. This year, there will be three Persons in the Godhead; next year, but One; and the third year, the Trinity will be restored, to hold its precarious sovereignty, until it shall be again dethroned by the worms of the dust it has made.

In these contests with conservative clergy Mann had the support of the law, the Board and, as we see above, his own considerable skill in defending a position. However, he realized quite well that the future of the common school rested ultimately in the hands of the populace. They would have to have faith in the schools and offer them their support. Fortunately, in Massachusetts the tide of clerical and lay opinion on religious matters was moving in a liberal direction. It was quite obvious to parents who visited the schools, examined the textbooks, and listened to the Bible readings that the spirit of Christianity was very much present. Besides, the possibility that Reverend Smith's brand of fire-and-brimstone Calvinism might be returned to the schools no doubt seemed to many to pose a more real and immediate threat than the claims that the Unitarians and atheists were attempting to win the children's allegiance. The day of the established church had passed in Massachusetts, and few wished to see its return in any guise. Then, of course, there were the Irish Catholics who were pouring into the state. It was deemed far better to agree on and plant a firm nonsectarian Protestantism in the public schools than to see a day when a plan of local option would establish the Catholic faith in those school districts where the Irish were settling in large numbers. Events in New York and Philadelphia furnished evidence of the need for Protestants to unite in the face of what was considered a Catholic threat to the common schools.

By 1830 the mass influx of Irish Catholics into the cities of the Northeast had begun. It would continue with increasing intensity through the forties. In New York City, Boston, and Philadelphia the Irish formed a conspicuous community within the larger community, complete with their own taverns, clubs, and newspapers. Also quite visible were the growing numbers of Catholic churches, priests, nuns, and parochial schools. To many citizens these immigrants represented yet another wave of newcomers to be welcomed for the contributions their labor would make to the development of the nation. Urban Democratic organizations eagerly enlisted them into the party as a new source of support at the polls. Assurances by Horace

Mann and other school leaders that education would Americanize foreign-born children apparently contributed to the optimism of the more sanguine native citizens and heightened their support of the common schools. But there were other Americans who looked at these developments in a quite-different light. To some, the foreigners represented an economic threat. One newspaper writer argued in 1844:

Our laboring men, native and naturalized, are met at every turn and every avenue of employment, with recently imported workmen from the low wages countries of the old world. Our public improvements, railroads, and canals are thronged with foreigners. They fill our large cities, reduce the wages of labor, and increase the hardships of the old settlers.

Still others saw, in the growing numbers of Catholics, a danger of far greater consequence. Two centuries after the wars of religion many Protestants continued to view the pope as an agent of Satan, determined to strike down every vestige of Protestantism and all republican institutions. To militant Protestants the masses of Catholic immigrants represented an army of destruction that had to be prevented from exerting an influence upon American life. One of the most virulent exponents of this point of view was the portrait painter and inventor Samuel F. B. Morse. His book, *Foreign Conspiracy Against the Liberties of the United States*, became a manual for anti-Catholic agitators. For Morse the "question of Popery and Protestantism, or Absolutism and Republicanism, which in these two opposite categories are convertible terms," was "fast becoming and will shortly be the great absorbing question, not only of this country, but of the whole civilized world."

During the 1830s anti-Catholicism manifested itself in a variety of ways. At times extremists impelled their audiences to violent acts such as the burning of the Ursuline Convent in Charlestown, Massachusetts in 1834. Less-frenzied bigots established the Native American Party in 1837, and, two years earlier, a New York City group organized a Protestant Association, whose primary function was to help defeat the Democratic friends of the Irish Catholics. The growing and highly visible Irish population of New York provided their foes numerous opportunities to demonstrate their hostility. One of the most dramatic issues involved schooling.

As noted in the first chapter, the bulk of the state school funds destined for New York City went to the Public School Society. This was a chartered philanthropic organization founded by Protestant laymen to provide elementary education for poor children. It was governed not by a publicly elected or politically appointed body but by a self-perpetuating board of trustees. Though not dominated by any single denomination, the climate and orientation of its schools were such that most Catholics felt they could not in good conscience send their children. Among their objections were the practice of reciting Protestant prayers and hymns, exclusive use of the King James Bible, and the employment of religious, literary, and historical texts displaying anti-Catholic biases, including the frequent use of the derogatory term "popery." With many Catholic parents boycotting the Society's schools and an insufficient number of parochial schools available, large numbers of New York City's children were totally without the benefits of education.

Interestingly, the Catholics found a champion of the school issue not among the Democrats but in the leader of the upstate, liberal faction of the Whig Party, Governor William Henry Seward. Unlike most politicians and reformers, who appear to have virtually ignored the Catholics' difficulties, Seward revealed an understanding of and a willingness to face up to the fact that what Protestants considered nonsectarian education was, to Catholics, quite the contrary. Sensitive to Catholic interests and expressing concern for the welfare of the state, Seward in 1839 and again in 1840 addressed the legislature in support of public aid to parochial schools.

Heartened by the governor's position, Catholics in the city, under the leadership of Bishop John Hughes, approached the

Board of Aldermen of the New York City Common Council requesting a share of the state school funds to help support seven of their schools. Citizens who saw in this a violation of the principle of church-state separation joined with the Public School Society, which feared decreased financial aid, and with outright bigots to oppose the move. Twice the Catholics petitioned, and twice they were denied. Caught between a desire not to antagonize their Irish supporters and an unwillingness to be an instrument of the Whig governor, the Democratic-controlled Council defended their action on the high and safe ground of separation of church and state.

In 1841 the battle of petitions and counterpetitions moved to Albany. Despite their setbacks in the city, the Catholics still had reason to hope for success. Governor Seward's willingness to support their cause had not diminished even though anti-Catholic sentiment in the state had turned against him at the polls in the election of 1840, causing him to fall well below his 1838 victory margin and to trail his party throughout the state. In his annual address to the legislature in January 1841 the governor suggested, for the first time, that the Catholic children might be served through public schools. An extension of this concept was included in a course of action presented to the legislature by Seward's close associate, the Whig Secretary of State and *ex officio* State Superintendent of Schools, John C. Spencer. Spencer advised that the district school system be at last extended into the city. The Public School Society would continue to run its institutions, even though they would officially be designated district schools. Residents who wished to establish public schools not under the Society's management could do so through a popular referendum in their districts. State funds theoretically would be limited to the support of secular education for all children. The inclusion of any religious teachings would be a matter to be determined and, if desired, supported exclusively by the district boards. Thus, in districts with Catholic majorities, the public schools could well have a Catholic orientation.

Bishop Hughes and his followers accepted the Spencer proposal, but the opposition was furious. Protest petitions, editorials and anti-Catholic tracts poured into the legislature, which responded by delaying action until the 1842 session. The political campaign during the fall of 1841 found the Whigs split over the Spencer plan and the Catholic Association of New York City presenting its own slate of candidates for the legislature. Ten of the Democratic candidates for Assembly seats supported the Spencer plan and thus also gained the nomination of the Catholics. But for the three remaining Assembly seats and the Senate positions the Catholic Association presented an alternative slate. None of the latter was elected, but the three anti-Spencer Assembly Democrats were defeated by Whigs.

At the next session of the legislature William Maclay, one of the Catholic Association's endorsed Democrats, was named chairman of the Assembly's school committee. He proceeded to successfully steer through his committee a bill incorporating the Spencer plan. Under his leadership the bill was passed in the lower chamber by a 64 to 16 vote margin. In the Senate the going was more difficult. Anti-Seward Whigs joined with the New York City Democrats who had been snubbed by the Catholic Association to oppose the measure. The bill ultimately was passed by a single vote. But before even this could be realized, an amendment of some significance was added. It stipulated that state funds were to be prohibited to all district schools in which "any religious sectarian doctrine or tenet shall be taught, inculcated, or practiced. . . ." Thus the original intent of the Spencer plan, which would have enabled the Catholics to introduce the tenets of their faith into the public schools of their districts, was defeated. In the long run the act also brought the demise of the Public School Society. It provided that the Society be allowed to continue managing its schools but under the general supervision of the elected city Board of Education, which was committed to fostering the growth of popularly controlled district schools. With both the

city Board and state legislature determined to discourage
further expansion of its schools, the Society shortly ended its
mission and deeded its property to the city.

So it was that the district system of public schooling came to
New York City. For the Catholic minority the price of sending
their children to these schools was high. Not only were their
clergy firmly attached to the principle that education devoid of
Catholic teachings was no education at all, but the so-called
nonsectarian public schooling demanded by law continued to
embrace practices that were antagonistic to Catholic beliefs.
Not the least of these was the daily reading from the King
James Bible. Exhausted from their battle, the Catholics of
New York ceased further agitation, taking a bit of consolation
from a partial victory. In Philadelphia, however, intense Catholic opposition to Protestant nonsectarianism in the public
schools raised temperatures on both sides so high as to make
the New York controversy seem like a Sunday school picnic.

By 1840 reformers had succeeded in solidly establishing a
common school system in Philadelphia. In 1837 it had been
declared that the "stigma of poverty" would no longer be
assigned under law to the public schools of the city and county.
The following year the state legislature took action to ensure
that public school children would be guided by Protestant
morality: "The Old and New Testaments, containing the best
extant code of morality, in simple, beautiful and pure language,
shall be used as a school book for Reading, without comment
by the Teacher, but not as a textbook for religious discussion."

The religious climate of the Philadelphia public schools was,
in nearly every respect, similar to that which existed in the
schools of New York's Public School Society. There were, however, some significant differences in the Philadelphia story.
Here, not only had Catholic children been chastised but Catholic teachers had been dismissed for their refusal to participate
in readings from the King James Bible and other religious
exercises. Also, Philadelphia's Catholics, led by Bishop Francis
Kendrick, sought from the city Board of Controllers funda-

mental changes in public school practices deemed offensive to their faith rather than funds to support separate parochial schools.

The response in January 1843 to Catholic requests was not wholly satisfactory to Bishop Kendrick. The Board expressed a willingness to hear specific complaints of failure to abide by its 1834 ruling prohibiting "the introduction or use of any religious exercises, books or lessons into the Public Schools." As for Bible reading—not embraced under the 1834 mandate— the Board announced that children might be excused should their parents so request. It also declared that any version of the Bible might be permitted in the schools so long as it did not contain notes or comments. However, since the Catholic Douay Bible did include annotations, it was, in fact, prohibited.

Some Philadelphia newspapers took violent exception to Kendrick's campaign and to what they interpreted as the soft-on-Catholics position of the Board. They insisted that the nation and its schools were essentially Protestant and should remain so. The Catholics were accused of attempting to drive the Bible from the school and "to subvert the foundation of our civil and religious institutions." The anti-Catholic "no popery" cause gained added' support with the founding in Philadelphia of the American Protestant Association in 1842 and the Republican Association the following year. Both organizations were viciously anti-Catholic, and both made common cause with opponents of change in traditional religious practices in the schools. Posters, tracts, editorials, and sermons were utilized to warn the citizens of the city of a Catholic threat to the schools. To ensure Protestant control of public education, demands were made that city and county school officials be popularly elected.

Bishop Kendrick had initially decided not to challenge the Board's ruling on the Bible issue, choosing instead to concentrate on calling for investigations of schools that peristed in holding religious exercises. By early 1844, however, his patience had worn thin in the face of intensified anti-Catholic campaigns. Rather than remain silent or modify his position, he became more aggressive. With the assistance of petitions from Catholic lay groups and editorials in the *Catholic Herald*, Kendrick pressured the Board to, in effect, either permit the use of the Douay Bible or discontinue Bible reading in the schools altogether. Caught in the middle, the Board declared its determination to enforce its earlier pronouncements regarding Bible reading, religious exercises, and textbooks. The Douay version was still ruled unacceptable, although provisions were made to excuse Catholic teachers from the task of leading Bible readings.

Neither side was pleased with the Board's stand, although Bishop Kendrick expressed a willingness to live with it. Accusations and name calling filled the air to the point where Philadelphia approached the brink of mass hysteria. On May 3, 1844 riots broke out between Protestant and Catholic mobs. On May 5, a Protestant youth was killed, and for the next week the city was a battleground. Catholic churches and schools were attacked and burned, and dozens of homes were put to the torch. Order was restored only after militia and regular army and navy forces were called to the scene. A grand jury investigation into the riots resulted in a report issued on June 15 that placed the blame on "the effort of a portion of the community to exclude the Bible from our Public Schools." The Catholics, of course, denied the charge, and the nativist (anti-foreign, anti-Catholic) press had a field day.

July 4 provided an ideal occasion for "100 percent Americans" to express their loyalty to flag and Bible and their abhorrence of so-called papist threats to both. The Independence Day parade was filled with banners bearing such slogans as "The Bible is the Basis of Education and the Safeguard of Liberty," "Foreign influence is one of the most baneful foes of a Republican Government," and "God and our Country." Patriotic bombast, Catholic fears, Protestant suspicions, and flying rumors blended perfectly that day to provide the spark of conflict. It was May 3 all over again, an entire weekend of mob action, gunfire, and the storming of a Catholic church. Once more troops were called in to restore the peace. This was to be the last outbreak of this kind. Responsible Catholics and Protestants alike joined in condemning mob violence. Bishop Kendrick abandoned his attempts to make the public schools more responsive to the sensitivities of Catholic youth and teachers and concentrated on expanding the diocesan school system.

Horace Mann, failing to take into account possible Catholic objections, had envisioned the nonsectarian Protestantism of the common schools as a force for social harmony. By the end of the 1840s there was wide support for his brand of religious-moral education. Unfortunately, the motivation for this was not always as humanely enlightened as was Mann's. Some of the most unbending sectarians, it seems, suddenly found wide areas of religious agreement when faced with Catholic claims and demands such as those put forth in New York City and Philadelphia. Setting aside the doctrines that divided them, between 1840 and 1860 they effectively united to ban state aid to parochial schools in New Jersey, Wisconsin, Michigan, Ohio, Indiana, Massachusetts, Iowa, Minnesota, and Kansas. In Massachusetts and Maine required reading of the King James Bible in public schools was established by law during the 1850s. By then the Catholics had become fully convinced that the common schools maintained a religious atmosphere threatening to the faith of their children. For them the only recourse was to hearken to Bishop Hughes' cry that every Catholic child be in a Catholic school.

The question of the role of religion in the common schools was by no means restricted to the Northeast. As the above list of states indicates, there was also concern west of the Appalachians over the threatened expansion of Catholic influence. Compounded with this was the fear of Protestant ministers that the very nature of a frontier wilderness contained forces hostile to ordered, Christian community life. The clerical missionaries who traveled westward to spread the gospel of salvation also preached in support of common schools. In numerous communities they took active leadership roles in the establishment and direction of public education. The new states of the West had never established official religions and, therefore, had no history of bitter struggles to separate church and state. As a result clergymen in this area tended to be less restrained than their Eastern colleagues about enjoining in political activities or holding civil offices. Throughout the Old Northwest ministers were employed as public-school teachers, county supervisors of education, and district superintendents of schools. The superintendents of public instruction for Indiana, Caleb Mills, and for Michigan, John D. Pierce, were ordained clergymen. Here as in the East the common schools were dedicated first and foremost to moral education. The teacher's role was defined as a holy one:

As certainly as God has traced this way for the development of the mind, so certainly the teacher should follow it in his method. The organization of the child's mind is not altered when he is sent to school; it remains the same. And as God was the teacher of the child til now, so he will remain his teacher, and the school-teacher ought to be his assistant. . . .

What more pleasant vision existed for a minister of the gospel than that of children in tax-supported schools under the guidance of teachers of sound moral character, who daily led their charges in Bible reading, prayers and hymns common to all Protestant creeds? By 1850 even the most popular school readers were viewed as solid contributors to the cause of Christian morality. Their author, William Holmes McGuffey, was a professor of moral philosophy and a Presbyterian minister in good standing. Surely the transfer of responsibility for elementary schooling from church to state had not wrought the dire consequences envisioned by some conservative clergy. In the face of urban and frontier dislocations, a powerful Catholic Church, and large waves of foreign immigrants stood the common school, bastion of Protestant morality, patriotic nationalism, and social order.

Winning the support of the clergy was extremely important for the cause of school reform. Through their sermons reluctant taxpayers and lethargic legislators were stirred to action. But clerical allies and popular support were by no means the total answer to realizing the objectives of common schooling. Once the textbooks had been obtained, the schoolrooms built, and the children assembled, the great burden would fall upon the shoulders of teachers. If they could not be won over to the cause of reform, or if they were not of the caliber to accomplish the mission of the school, all the efforts of reformers, politicians, and ministers would amount to little.

The crucial role of the teacher was expressed innumerable times by reformers. With moral development as the common school's primary goal, it was deemed absolutely essential that the teacher's character be of the highest repute. Horace Mann insisted that school committees must act as "sentinels stationed at the door of every schoolhouse in the State, to see that no teacher ever crosses its threshold, who is not clothed from the crown of his head to the sole of his foot, in garments of virtue." He was convinced that failure to secure virtuous teachers had been responsible for some of the most vile practices of the young:

If none but teachers of pure taste, of good manners, of exemplary morals, had ever gained admission into our schools, neither the school rooms, nor their appurtenances would have been polluted, as some of them now are, with such ribald inscriptions, and with the carvings of such obscene emblems, as would make a heathen blush.

Readers, take note. Another of our "serious" contemporary problems has roots deep in the past.

Among their several tasks, teachers were called on to implement the new methods that had so attracted reformers. At the heart of the progressive approach to education was the more-humane attitude toward children and child rearing so prominent in the writings of Rousseau, Franklin, and Pestalozzi. This approach gained increasing popularity in Jacksonian America. The spirit of democracy, liberal theology, Pestalozzianism, and phrenology contributed in varying proportions to the formulation of advice offered parents and teachers by such writers as Horace Mann, Lydia Sigourney, Jacob Abbott, Lyman Cobb, and Horace Bushnell. No less concerned with the religious and moral development of children than the most conservative Calvinists, these modernists called into question time-honored notions of infant depravity and innate human tendencies toward wickedness. They compared the child to a delicate young plant whose successful nurture could best be attained through slow, patient, and tender care. If tendencies toward depravity did in fact exist, then it was deemed far more sensible to follow Horace Bushnell's advice to carefully "weed out" sin rather than attempt to break the will with a rod. Neither plant nor child could flourish if treated roughly.

A proper environment for learning was declared essential. Place children in pleasant, healthful surroundings; expose them to examples of morality provided through Biblical and secular literature and the behavior of virtuous parents and teachers. Apply the rod only when gentler means of rational persuasion had failed, and then the child must be made aware by parent or teacher that "it hurts me more than it does you."

Beneath the liberal veneer of this modern approach to child nurture, it is not difficult to discern the perpetuation of some ancient objectives. When all was said and done, the child was to be not too different from what the Puritan forebears had desired their children to be: virtuous, obedient, thrifty, diligent, and loyal to faith and state. The line between reasoning with and preaching to children was often blurred. While the old emphasis upon fear and punishment was denigrated by the modernists, they seemingly had not lost sight of the effectiveness of guilt realization as a means of controlling behavior.

Today we can appreciate that the apparently gentler methods of the reformer could at times be more harmful to the child than more direct physical punishment. As historian Bernard Wishy observed, "Quick strong punishment, when justified, probably allows the child to feel he has paid his debts, while gentler methods in excess would keep the child's sense of guilt alive and active."

Still, when considered in the light of then prevailing attitudes, these reformers offered an optimistic outlook on human nature and a more humane approach to child nurture. The schools they were attempting to uplift were often staffed by incompetent teachers, social misfits who mollified their own frustrations by subjugating their charges to frequent lashings. One brutish teacher of the 1840s boasted of having whipped a dozen boys consecutively for not being able to discern the difference between "immorality and immortality." A coeducational school in Boston reported in 1844 an average of 130 floggings per day, this out of a total student population of 250. And there were many voices raised to defend such practices on grounds ranging from the innate depravity of man to the findings of "science." In an essay entitled "Corporal Punishment as a Moral Discipline," appearing in the *Southern Literary Messenger* in 1841, the author argued, "Flagellation is compendious and economical of time. It is refreshing—composes the wandering thoughts, brightens the wits, quickens the animal spirits and braces the nerves. It is a sort of Animal Magnetism, a galvanic battery—a thunderstorm to purify the moral atmosphere." One of the Reverend Smith's many charges against Horace Mann was that he discouraged corporal punishment. Other teachers and preachers proclaimed the sanctity of the rod, citing as support over 20 allusions to this form of punishment in the Bible.

One of the most colorful and highly publicized conflicts between the traditionalists and modernists occurred in Boston following the publication of Horace Mann's *Seventh Annual Report* (1843). Many of the city's teachers found Mann's enthusiasm for the methods of Prussian teachers as well as his aspersions against their own reliance upon the rod and dated teaching techniques a pill too bitter to swallow. A group of masters organized for battle, and 31 signed the "Remarks on the Seventh Annual Report . . . ," which proclaimed, in so many words, that the public schools of the state were good and getting better every day. Mann was rebuked for his espousal of newfangled methodology and reason-above-rod approach to discipline: "How careful should men of influence be to encouraging that excess love of freedom which can brook no restraint."

There followed a series of pamphlet exchanges between Mann and the teachers, carrying titles beginning with the words "Reply to the 'Remarks' . . . ," "Rejoinder to the 'Reply' . . . ," and "Answer to the 'Rejoinder' . . . ." Mann's political and literary skills proved superior to the teachers'. He carefully marshaled and manipulated facts and figures to arouse public indignation. He called attention to the fact that Boston teachers in many instances earned as much as twice the salary of their rural counterparts who, he claimed, were often more-effective instructors. Readers were reminded that the use of the rod was not restricted to punishing boys: "Would you whip the sensitive trembling girl, who comes to school effusive of sweet affections, and as inoffensive as the flowers which she brings as an offering to her teacher?" To counter charges that his attraction to Prussian school practices was cause to question his patriotism, Mann published a letter written to him by George Combe in which the noted phrenologist proclaimed, "You love what is good, and by elective affinity are attracted towards it, and draw it towards you, be it French, German, or American."

Mann's success was not so much in creating an opinion favorable to more humane forms of discipline as in focusing the attention of a public increasingly disposed to this point of view on practices in the schools. Corporal punishment did not disappear. In fact, Mann himself voiced approval of occasional use of the rod as a last resort, when all attempts at moral suasion had failed. This was the position adopted by the Boston school authorities, and its enforcement was one of the fruits of Mann's struggle with the schoolmasters. The beatings declined dramatically. By 1860 the average number of reported floggings in all of Boston's schools combined amounted to only 74. Whether the teachers themselves had been converted to the humanitarian position or whether their leniency was primarily the result of official policy supported by the requirement that detailed records of corporal punishments be maintained, cannot be determined.

It was important to win brushfire skirmishes such as that with the Boston schoolmasters. They provided a means of dramatizing the cause of the new education. However, in order to guarantee the accomplishment of reform on a large scale, a broad strategy was essential. The right people had to be enlisted into teaching; they had to be trained in the new techniques and indoctrinated with a sense of mission. As noted, school authorities were admonished by reformers to entrust their children to none but teachers of the most impeccable moral character. In view of the objectives of common schooling, no other requirement could be considered more important. How fortunate for school boards that women, traditionally paid less than men for performing the same jobs, were being heralded by such reformers as Pestalozzi, Mann, and Barnard as particularly suited to the task of teaching young children! Women, as members of the gentler, purer sex, could be more readily entrusted to properly guide children's moral development than those low-life men who so often dropped in and out of the teaching profession. Women were pronounced eminently suited to carry out the modern, more humane approaches to teaching. In their hands children could best be nurtured as tender shoots. Horace Mann explained that women "govern with less resort to physical force, and exert a more kindly, humanizing and refining influence upon the dispositions and manners of their pupils." Henry Barnard credited the large influx of female teachers into Rhode Island's schools as having "greatly improved the discipline, moral influence, and manners. . . ." Women were highly idealized in this romantic age, and consequently, much was expected of them:

Female Charm

I would have her as pure as the snow on
    the mount—
As true as the smile that to infamy's given—
As pure as the wave of the crystalline fount,
Yet as warm in the heart as the sunlight
    of heaven
With a mind cultivated, not boastingly wise,
I could gaze on such beauty, with exquisite
    bliss,
With her heart on her lips and her soul in
    her eyes—
What more could I wish in a dear woman than this.

While a few voices were raised on behalf of equal rights for women, the overwhelming number of women and men alike subscribed to the notion of a separate and unique role for the fairer sex:

What Are the Rights of Women?

The right to love whom others scorn,
The right to comfort and to mourn.
The right to shed new joy on earth,
The right to feel the soul's high worth.
Such women's rights, and God will bless
And crown their champions with success.

Faced with the costs of expanding school systems and assured by reformers that they were doing the right thing, school boards throughout the country welcomed female teachers. To get an idea of the bargain taxpayers received, in 1846 the average weekly salary for men teachers in rural areas was $4.00; women teachers received $2.53. In urban areas that same year it was $11.53 for men as opposed to $4.18 for women. Yet, for the spinsters of America it was a dream come true. How much more satisfying was the classroom and a chance for a modest income than a life as an unwelcome dependent in the home of a relative. Certainly, when faced with the other opportunities for employment open to women—making hats or clothing, working as domestics or in a factory—teaching appeared highly attractive. As one female educator commented in 1836, "The profession of teaching is, then, one which is open to those of our sex who are disposed to gain for themselves an honorable standing and support, to be useful in the world, and to cultivate the talents which God has given them."

While women marched in increasing numbers into the schoolrooms of America, the male teacher became more and more a rarity. Teaching, particularly on the elementary level, had never been accepted as a proper occupation for a red-blooded American man. In the 1840s and 1850s a burgeoning economy and expanding frontier offered numerous opportunities for men who might formerly have entered teaching only as a last resort. Even those to whom a career in education appeared attractive now found it more difficult to gain employment. Whether motivated primarily by the opinions of reformers or, more likely, by the dictates of the budget, school boards generally preferred to hire women. This dramatic reversal in a single generation was typified in Massachusetts, where the percentage of male teachers in the public schools fell from approximately 60 in 1840 to 14 in 1860. Figures for 1852 show that in Brooklyn 103 out of 108 public school teachers were women. In Philadelphia that same year women outnumbered men 699 to 82. In state after state the schoolmarm was in, the schoolmaster out.

Once the proper recruits were obtained, the next concern of the reformers was to develop an army of teachers passionately devoted to the cause of public education, committed to and competent in the new techniques of dealing with children and subject matter. The analogy of teachers to an army of recruits is by no means farfetched. As Merle Borrowman has pointed out, the teachers of this period were expected to be agents for implementing educational reforms, not their originators or directors. Leadership in education was viewed as appropriately belonging in the hands of well-educated laymen who sat on school boards or occupied positions in the educational bureaucracies of the several states.

To provide the kind of professional education considered essential for teachers, reformers promoted the normal school.* Many had visited Prussia and had been impressed with the quality of the graduates of her state teacher-training institutions. It made sense to these reformers that the desired increased state initiative in matters pertaining to schooling should extend to teacher preparation. As noted in the first chapter, such an idea had been advocated as early in 1824 by James G. Carter. He, and later Mann, looked with disfavor on the American scene, where the primary agencies for training teachers for the common schools were the private academies. A number of these institutions offered their tuition-paying students courses in the arts of school teaching. The reformers believed that as private institutions the academies simply lacked the commitment to serving "public purposes." Even more important, these schools were by no means totally devoted to teacher training, and neither were their student bodies. How could one be assured of dedication to public education among teachers prepared in private schools? How firm was the resolve to lifelong careers in teaching of those exposed to the academy's wide range of offerings? The advantage of state normal schools, it was argued, was that they would gather together youngsters fresh from the public schools and prepare them exclusively to return to the towns as common-

---

* The name of the institution stems from the Latin word "norm," meaning rule, thus a school for instructing in the rules of teaching.

school teachers. In the cloistered atmosphere of the normal school, young ladies would learn to master the elementary school subjects they would later teach. They would be instructed in the "art of teaching," school management, and the proper virtues and would have some opportunities for supervised practice teaching. Equally as important as the development of skills, the future teachers would be constantly reminded that theirs was a noble calling, one that required absolute dedication and perhaps even privation. The image of the teacher presented in professional literature of the day was that of a missionary carrying morality and knowledge to children, of a professional totally committed to her task and willingly obedient to the directives of principal, superintendent, and school board. One can only imagine how susceptible the young, impressionable females were to such sentiments as the following, which appeared in the *Massachusetts Teacher:*

> Mighty your office, teacher!
>> Higher than the kings of earth;—
> Are you not the prophet preacher,
>> To the future giving birth?

For Horace Mann the establishment of normal schools was part and parcel of the common-school crusade. He regarded them "as a new instrument of progress for the improvement of the human race." The public schools, he contended, could never become truly common until the more affluent members of society had enough faith in them to entrust their children to their care. To achieve this, public schools would have to surpass private institutions in terms of quality education. Mann was certain that success in meeting this challenge depended heavily upon a corps of outstanding teachers prepared in state normal schools.

As in so many areas of school reform, Massachusetts took the lead in establishing normal schools. The Boston-headquartered American Institute of Instruction helped promote the cause, which had been introduced almost singlehandedly by James Carter. By 1838 the movement had gained additional support from Governor Everett and the members of the recently formed state Board of Education, including its secretary, Horace Mann. Early that year Edmund Dwight, a wealthy member of the Board, offered to donate $10,000 to aid in the establishment of normal schools, if the legislature would appropriate an equal amount. The proposal was accepted, and on July 3, 1838 the first state normal school was opened in an old academy building facing the green in Lexington. In keeping with the Board's plan to establish three such institutions before the end of 1840, a second school at Barre began its work in September 1839 and a third at Bridgewater the following year.

With the opening of normal schools, school reformers were able to wage their campaign on yet another front. While Mann and his friends exerted pressure on the state government, local school boards, and the general public to accept the new concepts of schooling, teachers who were exposed to the modern techniques and ideology entered the classrooms. The textbooks used in the normal schools, including Alonzo Potter and George Emerson's *The School and the Schoolmaster* and David Page's *Theory and Practice of Teaching*, were explicit expositions of the views of leaders like Mann and Barnard. Indeed, Page drew heavily from Mann's *Annual Reports*, liberally quoting from them in the pages of his text. In the words of historian E. Douglas Branch, "Page's text, Mann's twelve *Reports*, and the volumes of Barnard's *Journal [American Journal of Education]* were the literary seeds of the modern profession."

In accordance with the wishes of the reformers, the early normal schools were "no-nonsense" institutions with only one purpose to fulfill: the training of common-school teachers. The curriculum was limited almost exclusively to that end. Students learned the "art of teaching" or "science of teaching" from books like Page's, through courses in mental and moral philosophy, and by practice teaching. The subject matter they studied was that which they would be required to teach in the common schools. Neither Latin nor Greek was included. The classics were for those preparing for college and eventual leadership roles in society, not for future teachers.

The state normal schools became one more target for those opposed to increased expenditures for education, centralization of control, progressive teaching methods, more lenient approaches to child nurture, and the secularization of the common schools. In 1840 a committee of the Democratic-controlled lower house of the Massachusetts legislature sought to stem the tide of what many insisted was the "Prussianizing" of the common schools. Its report called for the abolition of both the state Board of Education and the normal schools on the grounds that these institutions stood squarely in the way of local control of education and were "contrary in every respect, to the true spirit of our democratic institutions." Though the report reflected the positions of the Democratic party in Massachusetts and of Governor Marcus Morton, its proposals failed to secure passage in the legislature. The problem was that the Democrats could offer no viable alternatives to these institutions. While calling for democratization of politics by allocating greater power to local government, they were also fully committed to the common schools and, no less fervently than the Whigs, proclaimed its miraculous powers. Thoughtful Democrats might regret the direct participation of the state in maintaining normal schools, but they were forced to acknowledge that local communities were neither equipped nor willing to establish teacher-training facilities. And the propriety of private institutions preparing teachers for public schools was questionable. Ultimately the legislature acted to further the programs of the Board, including the development of normal schools.

Attacks against the normal schools surfaced again during Mann's controversy with the Boston schoolmasters in 1844 as well as during his several encounters with conservative clergy, but these institutions, like the common-school movement of which they were a part, survived. During the 1840s and 1850s normal schools came into being in various parts of the Northeast and West. By 1860 there were 12 in the nation; five years later there were 22.

Although these figures impressively attest to the growing acceptance of the normal school idea, they also make it quite evident that during this era only a minute fraction of the common-school teachers were trained in those institutions. School boards continued to recruit personnel who had studied pedagogy at the academies and, even more, those whose total preparation consisted only of having completed the common-school course of study. Educational leaders were determined to reach these (in their view) inadequately trained teachers. Periodicals, including Mann's *Common School Journal* and Barnard's *Connecticut Common School Journal*, and various reports and pamphlets emanating from offices of state superintendents, were among the earliest instruments for in-service training. Probably more effective were the teachers' institutes, which assembled pedagogues for periods ranging from a few days to several weeks to be inspired by eminent educationists, instructed in the latest techniques, and informed of the most modern materials. Henry Barnard conducted the first such institute in Connecticut in 1839. Following this the practice spread to New York in 1843, Rhode Island in 1844, and Ohio, Michigan, and Massachusetts in 1845. A significant consequence of these gatherings was the development of an *esprit de corps* among teachers, one manifestation of which was solid support of the goals of common schooling as articulated by the reformers. In a number of cases it was also at the institutes that plans were formulated to organize state teachers' associations.

By the 1850s active opposition by teachers to the views of reform leaders was a thing of the past. The journals of the state teachers' associations suggest that at least the leadership among the pedagogues had been completely won over, not only to the modern concepts of teaching and teacher training but also to the role that had been assigned them by the reformers. Although denied real power in educational policy making, the associations called upon their members to view themselves as leaders in the struggle to save the minds and morals of youth from the pitfalls of an increasingly materialistic and complex society. In the light of their recent militancy we sometimes forget how, with hardly a murmur of resentment, teachers for generations accepted pitifully low salaries and severe restrictions on behavior that did not conform to the letter of Puritan-like morality. The only demands they in turn made on society were that it recognize the saving power of education and acknowledge the nobility of the teaching profession. The reformers, texts on teaching, normal school sermons, and educational journals proved remarkably effective in creating a missionary self-image among teachers, which was no less significant for the cause of school reform than successful efforts to achieve broad-based public and political support.

To discuss educational issues in a handful of states can only serve to provide dramatic examples of the kinds of struggles in which reformers were engaged throughout the land. Massachusetts, New York, and Pennsylvania certainly had no monopoly on religious controversy surrounding the schools. For instance, California in the 1850s was subject to the spectre of nativism and virulent conflicts over Bible reading and state aid to denominational schools. The cry of "Prussianizing the schools" was raised in state after state when reformers attempted to enhance the supervisory roles of state, county, and town governments and subsequently weaken the power of the local school districts. Advocates of state supervision in Ohio, for example, were not as successful as their counterparts in Massachusetts in staving off attacks. The state superintendent of schools, an office created in 1847, was abolished three years later, not to be reestablished until 1853. Conflicts abounded in every state in which the common-school goals were put forth. But by the middle 1860s throughout the North and West the reformers had won major battles. Their successes were not always as complete as they wished. At times two steps forward were followed by one step back; the availability, quality, reputation, and degree of acceptance of the established public schools varied within and among the states. However, the essential outcome was certain: the common school was here to stay.

Three decades of progress in public elementary schooling in Massachusetts testify to one of the most successful reform movements. In 1834, even prior to the establishment of the state Board of Education, the legislature took a step in asserting direct state participation in common school reform by establishing a school fund to be apportioned to the towns on condition that they tax themselves to the extent of providing one dollar per pupil each year. The same spring of 1837 that witnessed the creation of the Board also brought legislative response to the rising rate of child labor in the mills of the state. An act was passed requiring children to attend school for 3 months during the 12 months preceding their employment in factories. By today's standards this measure seems to present the smallest barrier to the evils of child labor. The fact is, however, that in those early days of industry the employment of children was in itself not considered necessarily undesirable. Horace Mann's views on the subject were rather typical of the opinions of humanitarians of his day. By exposing children to education, their labor in the factory, he believed, would be "converted from servitude into a useful habit of diligence."

As might be expected, it was during Mann's tenure as secretary to the Board that the towns of Massachusetts underwent the most dramatic changes in their common schools. State appropriations for education and local school taxes more than doubled. Over $2 million was expended on building new schoolhouses and on improving the old. School libraries became common and blackboards were introduced as an aid to teaching. Children found their school year lengthened considerably, and teachers' paydays became more pleasant as salaries rose by more than 50 percent. The quality of education was served not only by the state's involvement in school matters but also by the transfer of a good deal of controlling power from the local districts to the towns' school committees. While Mann's departure from the Board virtually marked the end of an era of leadership by Massachusetts in the common-school crusade, in 1852 the state offered one more significant innovation. That year it passed the first compulsory attendance law. Under its provisions children between the ages of 8 and 14 were required to attend school at least 12 weeks per year; no fewer than 6 weeks were to be continuous. In point of fact this initial law had so many loopholes that its enforcement was nearly impossible. The real importance of the measure was the precedent it set for the enactment of compulsory attendance laws in every other state of the union by 1918.

Another New England state deserving our particular attention is Rhode Island. Unlike her sister states she inherited no public-school tradition emanating from a Puritan colonial past. Founded by men driven for reasons of conscience from theocratically oriented Massachusetts, Rhode Island through the years resisted the establishment of ties both between state and church and state and school. Ironically, by 1840 the state's liberal tradition had been replaced by a more recent history of political conservatism which, among other things, was marked by a severe property limitation on the right to vote. Protests against this led in 1842 to a civil uprising known as the Dorr War. Although the insurrection was quashed and its leader Dorr sentenced to life imprisonment,[1] the conservatives were shaken. Suffrage was considerably extended, and public schooling was advocated as a contributor of many benefits, including respect for property and law and order. In 1843 Henry Barnard was called from Connecticut to act as agent for promoting and developing quality public education. Before retiring from the position in 1849, Barnard was instrumental in establishing throughout the state a system of free, public common schools.

---

[1] Dorr was released after serving one year of his sentence.

In 1845 he had told Rhode Island's legislators that it was the responsibility of civilized men to decide for the urban poor how best to raise them from barbarism. In response to this and other of his arguments, that body passed a school act that Horace Mann applauded as promising to give Rhode Island "one of the best systems of public instruction in the world." The abolition of the rate-bill was accomplished in 1848, decades ahead of similar actions by such states as Connecticut and New York, whose commitments to public education were far older. An interesting sidelight to the Rhode Island story is that, separated by a span of only a few months, the cause of public education had been espoused first by rebel leaders of the Dorr War and workingmen's party veteran Seth Luther and subsequently by Henry Barnard, moderate reformer and spokesman for Rhode Island's "establishment."

The state's role in the supervision of education had been established in New York as early as 1812. Here both Democratic and Whig administrations generally supported the improvement and expansion of the common schools and auxiliary services. In 1834 state funds were appropriated to support classes in pedagogy at one academy in each of the eight judicial districts. In 1844 the first state normal school opened at Albany. As we have previously seen, the common-school system finally took root in New York City in 1842. However, there remained one serious obstacle to a state-wide system of free public education: the rate-bill.

During the 1840s, 1850s, and into the 1860s, legislative attempts were made to establish in New York a policy of "free and gratuitous education" supported by local property taxes supplemented by state grants. Opponents of the scheme argued that the school tax was an unfair infringement on the rights of private property—taking one's personal assets to be employed in the education of other people's children. This was a powerful argument in a generation not far removed from the Revolutionary War. Had not the protection of the sacred rights of property been a large part of what was involved in the struggle with Britain? In New York, indeed in every state, the proponents of the common school were severely challenged to provide counterarguments. And, when effective answers to the "defense of property" position were forthcoming, they were often reprinted widely. Such was the case of Thaddeus Stevens' famous defense of the Pennsylvania school tax in 1835 and Horace Mann's *Fifth* and *Tenth Annual Reports.*[2] The reformers' appeals to men of property and wealth ranged from self-interest to social responsibility. They were reminded that an educated citizenry would be less likely attracted to the promises of radical schemes, and that educated workers were more apt to be efficient, obedient, and respectful of authority. Horace Mann and others described education as a natural right as sacred as the right to hold private property. Mann urged men of means to acknowledge their debts to previous generations and their responsibilities to generations to come. According to his arguments, an individual's wealth had been created in large part by the utilization of knowledge and resources developed in the past and passed on through a process of education. Neither knowledge nor the wealth that is the product of that knowledge is to be considered the possession solely of an individual or group of individuals. "The successive holders of this property are trustees, bound to the faithful execution of their trust by the most sacred obligations." As trustees it was incumbent upon them to employ their wealth in a manner that would ensure that knowledge would be transmitted to the rising generation. Thus, the school tax—instead of an infringement on individual rights—was a device through which the "holders of property" could meet their obligations.

The opponents of compulsory school taxation slowly lost ground in New York. In 1849 and 1851 the state legislature passed acts mandating local school taxes. Yet even as late as

---

[2] In 1842 the friends of public education in New York secured funds from the legislature to reprint and distribute 18,000 copies of Mann's *Fifth Annual Report.*

1851 districts were directed by the state to resort to the rate-bill in meeting the cost of teachers' salaries in excess of the amounts provided by the property tax and state school funds. Not until 1867 was the rate-bill finally abolished.

Of the major Northeastern states none had been less committed to the common-school idea prior to 1830 than Pennsylvania. There the practice of separate schooling along class and religious lines was firmly entrenched. Beginning in 1830 Governor George Wolf, supported largely by citizens of New York and New England origins, launched a reform drive. The going was difficult as opposition stiffened among rural farmers and property owners opposed to school taxes, religious groups with heavy financial and moral commitments to sectarian schools, and Germans determined to protect and promote their language and culture in their own schools. In Pennsylvania one could hear articulated every argument for and against the major elements of common-school reform.

The first small victory for the common-school forces was the establishment of a state school fund in 1830. A second break-through came in 1834. Under the leadership of Thaddeus Stevens "AN ACT to establish a General System of Education by Common Schools" was successfully steered through the legislature. The act granted shares of the state school fund to those counties that were willing to tax their citizens for the support of common schools. Nothing was included of a compulsory nature. Counties that chose not to participate would continue to be governed by the provisions of the Law of 1809, which mandated educational support only for children of the poor.[3] Yet, the reaction from rural areas and religious bodies was fierce. Many of the legislators who had supported the bill were later to lose their seats because of their vote. In 1835 only the concerted efforts of Thaddeus Stevens and his associates staved off an attempt to repeal the legislation. It was on

[3] In 1837 Philadelphia declared its public schools "now open to any child," thus absolving them from the "stigma of poverty."

this occasion that Stevens delivered his famous address in defense of public education. Reprinted throughout the land in his own time, and found in complete or partial form in innumerable texts to this day, the speech dramatically summarized the hopes and dreams of the common school advocates. Upon his death in 1868, Stevens was eulogized as the father of the Pennsylvania public schools:

Not a child in Pennsylvania, conning his spelling book beneath the humble rafters of a village school, who does not owe him gratitude; not a citizen rejoicing in that security which is found only in liberal institutions, founded on the equal rights of all, who is not his debtor.

The successful defense of the School Law of 1834 by no means signalled the end of the struggle. In 1837–1838, at the state constitutional convention, opponents of the common-school movement were able to block attempts to include a universal free-school article in the final document. Even by 1866 approximately 6000 children in the state were deprived of a public school education because the leaders in 23 districts chose not to accept the provisions of the School Law. However, far more significant is the fact that, by that year, 964 districts had utilized local taxes and state funds to provide systems of free common schools. Dramatic appeals by prominent figures like Thaddeus Stevens supplemented by the persistent efforts of countless local reformers had achieved nearly complete victory.

The history of the common-school movement in the West in many ways parallels that of the older settled areas. Similar arguments were aired over such issues as centralization of control, property taxes, rate-bills, and the like. But there were also some significant differences. The rapidly growing Western states had no indigenous historical precedents in education upon which to build. Educational traditions and attitudes toward reform were brought into the new lands by the settlers. The more heterogeneous the population with regard to places of origin, the more confusing the picture. In the end the rapidity and thoroughness with which the common school, this "Yankee device," was established usually depended on the strength of the New England influence. In state after state, where New Englanders settled, a common-school movement was instituted, teachers' associations were organized, and school journals were published. In state after state the leaders of educational reform and state superintendents were, more often than not, transplanted New Englanders. Local newspapers and the publications of teachers' organizations and state educational agencies kept Westerners abreast of reform activities in the East. Railroads brought Horace Mann and Henry Barnard to preach the gospel of reform and transported local leaders to inspect for themselves the "wonders" of the New England common schools. Back East the missionary spirit offered support for the crusade. The National Board of Popular Education, founded by Catherine Beecher, recruited hundreds of young schoolmarms for the new states. So taken with the spirit of reform was Governor Slade of Vermont that on at least one occasion he personally escorted a group of female teachers to Illinois.

In the West doubts and suspicions surrounding the New England import and opposition to school taxes were ultimately overcome by skillful appeals to pride and prejudices. Mastery of the basic three Rs was depicted not only as the best guarantee of personal success but as a necessary ingredient to frontier democracy. Private schools were described as bastions of a European type class system, whereas the common school, as one proponent put it, "ramifies itself into all parts of society— imparting wholesome knowledge to every child in the country." The future glory of the new states, it was argued, was dependent on a system of free schools the equal of, if not superior to, those in the East. Added to these appeals were others heard throughout the nation, stressing the moral power of education and the need to integrate immigrant children into the American value system.

A brief review of significant events in some key states illustrates the course of common-school reform in the West. In Ohio as well as Massachusetts 1837 marked the effective beginning of moves to extend the state's role in public-school supervision. A legislature dominated by New Englanders that year passed a bill creating a state superintendent of schools with powers and responsibilities similar to those granted Horace Mann in the Bay State. Samuel Lewis, the first to hold the office, was originally from Falmouth, Massachusetts. The following year the legislature acted to provide for a school census, a common-school fund, and a county tax of two mills. Also, in an effort to weaken district control that was typically synonomous with educational inertia, a modicum of supervisory responsibility was granted county and township authorities.

Though off to a good start, Ohio's reform forces had by no means achieved total success. In 1840 opponents of centralized authority struck back, abolishing the office of state superintendent and transferring his duties to the secretary of state. It took 13 long years of propaganda and political infighting led by citizens largely from the New England-oriented Western Reserve section of the state to regain the initiative for reform. The outcome was well worth the effort. Legislation in 1853 reestablished the state superintendency, levied a state school tax, and abolished the rate-bill. Ohio had achieved a statewide system of free common schools.

In Illinois in 1855, 28 years after the legislature had virtually destroyed the roots of a common-school system, reform forces won a long sought after victory. A free-school law was passed that provided a firm foundation upon which a common-school system would be erected. As historian John Pulliam convincingly points out, the influx of Easterners into northern Illinois played a major role in the development of popular support for school reform.

Neighboring Michigan came into the Union in 1837 with a constitutional acknowledgment of education as a state responsibility and a provision for the establishment of a state school office.

That same year a school law was passed authorizing state and local school taxes and establishing the position of state superintendent with general supervisory powers. By 1865 the only obstacle to a true system of free common schools in Michigan was a rate-bill. While Detroit had eliminated this device in 1842, statewide abolition did not occur until 1869.

Turning to the Pacific West, California entered the Union with constitutional provisions for a common-school system, including an elected state superintendent, but with no real structure for financial support. Throughout the 1850s school development in rural areas was hindered by a shortage of funds, while in San Francisco the schools were racked by controversy involving religious exercises in which nativists and anti-Catholics played their ugly roles. An educational breakthrough came in 1862 with the election of John Swett as state superintendent. Swett, who had been a teacher in Massachusetts and New Hampshire, not only recognized the necessity of teacher support in any program of educational reform but was extremely effective in organizing the profession as a political force. Using a teachers' institute like a political convention, he fired his audience with enthusiasm and sent them back to their districts to lobby for improved schooling. During Swett's tenure state, county, and local school taxes became the rule, and funds were provided to support a free school system, teacher training programs, school libraries, and a longer school year. By the end of the 1860s California provided a model of state commitment to the furtherance of public education.

Here and there in the North and West were exceptions to this pattern of success stories. Indiana, for example, lagged well behind her sister states of the Midwest. There constitutional support of public education backfired to inhibit the expansion of free schools. Variances in the amount of taxes collected by the several districts in the state were found by the courts to be incompatible with the constitutional mandate for a "uniform system of common schools." Thus all local school taxes were declared unconstitutional. Until 1867 the districts were forced to depend on the state school fund, which could support only two months of schooling per year, plus the rate-bill.

In New England, where the story began, Connecticut, despite her early school beginnings, slackened the pace of educational reform during the 1840s and 1850s. The state's school fund, fed by the sale of public lands, had always been one of the fattest in the nation. This tended to provide the kind of security that resulted in a reluctance by many local districts to tax themselves sufficiently to provide quality universal schooling. Despite his many efforts as legislator and state superintendent to enhance the state's supervisory role and to improve teacher training and schooling in general, Henry Barnard had to report, in 1855, that "a vast number of children among us are growing up without intellectual and moral culture necessary to make them industrious, respectable, law-abiding citizens." Not until the next decade was a free common-school education available to all Connecticut youth.

By 1865 systems of common schooling had been established throughout the northern, midwestern and western states. While in some areas, as we have noted, totally free, tax-supported schooling had not yet been fully realized, even opponents of reform must have known what was just over the horizon. The South, however, provides a different picture. Despite the existence of sentiment for common schooling, by 1850 it had become clear that the states below the Mason-Dixon Line had chosen to travel a separate road in search of distinct social and cultural objectives. Therefore, as a section apart the educational developments in the South will be discussed separately, in a later chapter.

The common schools of the period varied in terms of size, organization and curricula depending on their location. In rural areas, where the majority of Americans lived, one would most likely find the one- or two-room schoolhouse in which a pupil's progress was marked not by annual movement from one grade to the next but by his completion of one text and beginning of the next in the series. Only in larger towns and cities had grading been introduced. As for the course of study, in rural districts and regions governed by the frontiersman's distrust of too much "book larnin" frequently little was offered beyond the three Rs. Ohio did not mandate grammar and geography until 1848. Prior to this the directors of many school districts in the state actually forbade the teaching of anything but reading, writing, and arithmetic. In Massachusetts, on the other hand, efforts to broaden the curriculum met with some success. By 1850, in addition to the three Rs, state law required the teaching of English grammar, geography, orthography, and manners. Furthermore, a number of towns' schools also taught history and bookkeeping. Boston had introduced music into the curriculum as early as 1838, and beginning in 1845 its students were also able to elect natural philosophy and astronomy. One might find it surprising that it was in staid Boston with its Puritan heritage that music first appeared in the schoolroom. However, acceptance of the subject was granted for no light or frivolous reasons. Among the virtues attributed to its study were the quickening of "memory, comparison, attention, intellectual faculties," the fostering of "happiness, contentment, cheerfulness, tranquility," and "when not carried to excess [vocal music] must expand the chest and thereby strengthen the lungs and vital organs." We note that the study of music in Boston's schools embraced singing but most definitely not dancing. As a report of the Boston School Board declared, "Music has an intellectual character which dancing has not, and above all, music has its moral purposes which dancing has not." By 1865 the common schools of most of the nation's larger cities had followed Boston's example and introduced music into the classrooms.

Textbooks provide another indicator of the subjects taught in the common schools. By the 1860s schoolbooks appearing nationwide in the largest quantity and variety were readers, spellers, arithmetics, grammars, histories, and geographies. Regardless of the emergence of natural science, government, and drawing courses in some school systems, expansion into these areas was really a post-Civil War phenomenon.

Although reformers deplored the overemphasis upon rote learning and the system of prizes and medals that rewarded students for their ability to regurgitate facts at the expense of real understanding, these practices dominated the majority of classrooms during the period. Then, as now, current teaching techniques lagged well behind progressive educational ideals. For the teacher facing children of varying ages and levels of learning, recitation and drill seemed the most sensible way to provide order as well as the most expeditious approach to storing the minds with required moral preachments and essential knowledge. Despite this, the school experiences of children during these decades were quite likely to have been more pleasant than those of their predecessors. As previously noted, attitudes toward youth and childhood had been changing significantly over the recent decades. Whereas children were once judged little sinners, a blend of reason and romanticism led them now to be deemed tender seedlings to be lovingly nurtured. True, the rod did not disappear from the classroom, but its use became considerably more restrained. And though schoolmarms could be harsh taskmasters, there were fewer bullying brutes among them than among their male counterparts.

Schoolbooks, too, became more bearable as their authors responded to the modern educational outlook. In textbooks like those extremely popular readers of William Holmes McGuffey, children continued to be taught the lessons of morality and patriotism, but the stern, direct preachments of earlier schoolbooks were replaced or supplemented by stories and essays designed to appeal to youthful interests. "Children's literature prior to 1830," E. Douglas Branch notes, "had been didactic without guile." However, in later years, "with the sulphur reduced to a trace, the little dears actually liked the tonic. . . ." School readers tended to be eclectic, ranging far afield for material both interesting and of instructional value. Goldsbury and Russell's *The American Common-School Reader* of 1844, for example, included essays and speeches by such notable contemporary political figures as Edward Everett, Daniel Webster, John Quincy Adams, and Henry Clay, excerpts from the writings of Longfellow, Wordsworth, Bryant, Irving, Whittier, Shakespeare, Milton, and others, and passages from the Bible and from the sermons of well-known ministers of the day. Children's books designed for home reading consisted largely of works of fiction in which youthful heroes and heroines like Jacob Abbott's Little Rollo engaged in all sorts of adventures, the outcomes of which were certain to involve the triumph of morality.

Historians have given due credit to new and improved modes of transportation and communication as crucial factors in the welding together of our vast and diverse nation. However, it fell to Professor Ruth Miller Elson in her excellent study of nineteenth-century textbooks (*Guardians of Tradition*, Lincoln, Nebraska, 1964) to convincingly illustrate the vital force of schoolbooks, which "both created and solidified American traditions." Surpassed only by the Bible in readership, these products of predominantly New England authors presented to children throughout the land all that was generally accepted as useful and proper to know and believe. In his grammars, spellers, readers, geographies, and arithmetics the young scholar was assured that his world had been created by God exactly as depicted in the Bible to be the abode of man, that Christianity— particularly the Protestant brands—was the one true religion, and that the United States had been divinely favored and was surely the best and most glorious of all nations. There is nothing like a low opinion of others to reinforce pride in that which is yours. Antebellum textbooks, while often urging toleration of other peoples and beliefs, were quite specific in describing the "lower" levels in the hierarchy of nations, races, and religions. Today's whispered stereotypes of such groups as Catholics, Negroes, Jews, Orientals, Indians, Italians, and Mexicans were all quite vividly portrayed.

In their textbooks American youth were cautioned time and

again that the bestowal of God's blessings upon individuals and nations alike was dependent upon continued adherence to His code of virtue and morality. Indeed, examination of these texts reveals a quite apparent response to the promise of reformers that moral development was to be the chief goal of the common school. The works of major and minor literary, political and theological luminaries were gleaned to find moral lessons effectively presented. All the national heroes, led by the saintly Washington, were depicted as pillars of virtue. Industry, honesty, frugality, perseverence, and obedience to authority, it was promised, would bring God's material gifts. As one speller asserted, "In this country the way for a poor little boy to become a great and happy man is to be honest, industrious and good." On the other side of the coin, "Poverty is the fruit of idleness," and, "Declining prosperity is the usual attendant of degenerate morals in individuals, families, and in larger communities."

One would be laboring in vain if he sought to find in these texts any indications of dissatisfaction with the nature of American society. Readers were assured that the Revolution and Constitution had brought freedom and opportunity to all. Class divisions were natural and beneficial: "Society, when formed, requires distinctions, diversity of condition, subordination of ranks, and a multiplicity of occupations, in order to advance the general good." If an individual was unhappy with his lot, he was instructed to look no further than his own conduct for redress. As stated in Webster's *Reader* of 1835,

Hence the poor have no right to complain, if they do not succeed in business. They all enjoy the same rights; and if they continue in poverty, it is usually for want of industry, or judgement in the management of their affairs, or for want of prudence and economy in preserving what they earn. They have no more right to invade the property of the rich, than the rich have to invade the rights of the poor.

Such were the views presented in the schoolbooks read by generations of American youth. Conservative in their loyalties to the established system of beliefs and practices, yet boldly optimistic in their faith that through this system the most just society on earth was evolving, the textbook authors represented one more arm of common-school reform. They, too, believed that dangers to national unity and social harmony impending in such phenomena as urbanism, industrialism, sectionalism, and immigration could be checked by placing all the children of all the people together in schools. There a brotherhood of citizenship could be formed through lessons and experiences shared in common, a brotherhood that would remain firm despite later disparities in stations of life.

chapter four

beyond the common school

The wave of enthusiasm for education, with its seemingly boundless potential to serve the interests of man and society, found its greatest expression in the common-school movement. But it was by no means limited to this endeavor. During these years, 1830–1865, academies and colleges experienced dramatic growth, and entirely new forms of education appeared, informal as well as institutional. Not only were there efforts to meet the moral, intellectual, and vocational needs of the school-age population; considerable attention was also devoted to preschoolers and adults. Like the innumerable varieties of patent medicines, learning in its several forms was peddled as a great nostrum of the age.

At the outset of the period the academy was already established as the predominant institution of secondary education. The next 20 years witnessed the time of its greatest numerical growth and spread across the nation. In 1855 Henry Barnard counted 6185 academies enrolling a total of 263,096 students. But these figures are generally considered to have been below the mark. It was simply impossible to obtain an accurate count. Schools that were designated as colleges, seminaries, or institutes were often, in fact, private secondary schools, similar in every respect to institutions calling themselves academies. Academies in more remote regions often were founded, flourished for brief periods, and eventually failed without their existence being acknowledged by the record keepers.

It is equally difficult to arrive at a simple definition of an academy. They were a mixed bag of institutions. Among them were coeducational schools, female seminaries, and all-male academies. Though most offered both college preparatory courses and a terminal English curriculum, and many provided courses in pedagogy, a few limited their studies exclusively to those prescribed for entrance to the major Eastern colleges. In the South a number of postsecondary level military academies appeared, and of course there were the government-sponsored military and naval academies at West Point and Annapolis. Public and private normal schools were also generally considered academy-level institutions. Fortunately, Theodore Sizer has identified two distinguishing characteristics of most academies that, despite the obvious exceptions, are most helpful in discussing these schools and setting them apart from the colonial Latin grammar schools and the public high schools of a later day: in terms of control, they were relatively private; in terms of curricula, their offerings were broader and more practical than those of the Latin grammar school.

In innumerable ways the academy movement reflected the spirit of Jacksonian America. During the course of the eighteenth and early nineteenth centuries the public Latin grammar schools had been nearly totally rejected by taxpayers as aristocratic institutions fostering irrelevant education. Even in Massachusetts the number of these schools had dwindled to a handful by 1830. This was an age of enterprise; to gain popular support an educational venture, no less than a business venture, would have to hold out some prospect of solid, practical results. It would have to be sold. Mann, Barnard, and other proponents of common-school reform were quite aware of this and, fortunately, were equal to the task. However, until their victories were secured, few of these men sought and fewer still had much success in gaining public approval for tax-supported schooling on the secondary level. Though some secondary schools were established under church auspices, the primary area of educational interest among the several religious groups was collegiate. In fact, the most energetic, most successful proponents of secondary education during these years were neither social reformers nor religious leaders but prosperous farmers, professionals, and middle-class entrepreneurs. While very definitely concerned with the broad spiritual and social ramifications of education, these latter-day sons of Benjamin Franklin were also motivated by more immediate, utilitarian considerations. An academy would provide a useful education for the middle-class youngseter; an academy would add distinction to its locale.

With a board of trustees made up of solid citizens and, with luck, a corporate charter and financial assist from the state, the academy was "in business." The state's role was consistent with the prevailing practice of incorporating and financially aiding private ventures that were deemed beneficial to the public welfare. This was done for such enterprises as canals, banks, and medical societies, as well as for, in historian James McLachlan's words, "thousands of academies almost spontaneously organized by education-hungry Americans from one end of the nation to the other."

The extent of state aid in terms of both initial and supplementary grants varied, but no private academy could depend upon this source for primary support. Tuition was essential. The degree of state supervision of the academies also varied from state to state. New York, with its system of state inspectors and its requirements that academies offer instruction in pedagogy and college preparatory courses, exemplified a particularly high degree of involvement. However, in New York, as in every state, the principle of *laissez faire* prevailed. The academies were free to extend their offerings to include whatever was deemed appropriate by the trustees. Generally, if there was a wide-enough demand for a course, it was provided.

No better evidence of the optimistic faith in the power of

education exists than the great variety of courses available in these schools, usually offered in six-week packages. An 1837 report of the New York Regents reveals that no fewer than 60 different courses were being taught in the academies of the state, including architecture, Biblical antiquities, Chaldee, conchology, embroidery, extemporaneous speaking, Greek, Hebrew, Italian, Latin, nautical astronomy, phrenology, physiology, and waxwork. Despite the appearance of some rather exotic courses, most of the academies provided the traditional classical curriculum and such useful and "sensible" subjects as modern languages, natural science, English composition and literature, surveying, and bookkeeping. It was, therefore, quite possible at most academies to prepare for college admission. In fact, though the academy provided a terminal education for most of its students, it was also the leading source of college matriculants throughout the period. A number of schools brought order out of the chaos of multiple courses and varying student educational objectives by establishing a track system that provided choices among two or more programs, such as the classical or college preparatory, the English or general, and the normal or teacher training.

Regardless of the widespread enthusiasm for the academy movement, for several reasons the schools were by no means accessible to a majority of the nation's youth. During an era when the value of even a common-school education was doubted by many, advanced schooling was considered totally unnecessary by a significantly larger number of parents, particularly from the lower strata of society and the more remote regions of the country. Even families favorably disposed toward the academy often found it impossible to send their children. In a small shop or on a farm the absence of an adolescent son or daughter could result in a serious loss of useful labor. Also to be considered were the tuition charges and for many youngsters the costs of board and room in a private home in the vicinity of the school. Lodging in this manner was quite common. Academies, although most often situated in or near towns, drew students from the distant surrounding areas. Few maintained dormitories, and those that did were able to accommodate only a small fraction of their out-of-towners. At roughly $1.50 per week, living away from home proved a luxury that, as Professor Sizer states, "only the reasonably well-off could afford."

Those able to attend must have found the prospect truly exciting. Here was an opportunity to venture away from the confines of the family and to engage in studies that promised to be more challenging and meaningful than the district school rudiments. For some the academy represented the road to college. Others sought to round off the rough edges, to gain the veneer of culture and store of useful knowledge that seemed to offer the best provisions for a successful life career and status in society. Parents must have received some satisfaction from their ability to provide their children with educational opportunity beyond the common kind. Concern for their physical and moral welfare was probably lightened by the knowledge that the academies established rigid codes of conduct and were careful in approving homes in which students boarded. An alumnus of Phillips Exeter Academy, class of 1833, recalled that his classmates "boarded in good families in the town and were under good influences. They were treated as members of the family and subject to its discipline. If there was trouble in the house, the head of the family usually settled it without carrying it to the faculty."

After a period in attendance many students likely discovered that the reality of the academy experience was something less than the promise. The mark of the successful scholar was often not his understanding and appreciation of the subject but, instead, his ability to repeat by memory what he had read. True, this had been the method employed in secondary schools and colleges for generations, but by the middle of the nineteenth century the wastefulness of this approach and the availability of more meaningful techniques had been widely proclaimed by educational reformers. At first glance it appears ironic that the academies, which in their curricula were innovative often to excess, should have remained so conservative in their approach to teaching. But, in fact, the two conditions went hand in hand. Their numerous offerings appeared to represent their greatest resource and attraction. Lacking the finances to even consider employing a large staff of experts in the several fields, the textbook assumed the role of true master of the classroom. The recent technical revolution in printing and book publishing played a considerable role in the academy movement.

As the years passed, criticism of the academies intensified. In addition to inflated curricula, inadequate staffing, and outdated methods, detractors pointed out that these so-called "people's colleges" were beyond the reach of capable but poor children. As several of the academy towns expanded, it became more difficult for school authorities to watch over students once they left the campus. Parents often voiced concern that the boarding house arrangements were no longer protecting their children from the evil temptations of an urban environment. Yet, it was not the criticism that caused the academy movement to peak in the 1850s and begin a rapid decline after the Civil War. After all, what system or form of education has ever deserved to be graded excellent in all respects? What actually led to the academy's demise were its successes, the things it was praised for, that is, the provision of a form of secondary education offering programs deemed relevant to the lives of all youth, whether their futures lay in college and the professions, in business or the trades, or in the home as housewives and mothers. When the time arrived for civic leaders to declare such an education essential for all and in the public interest, the high school materialized. Few private academies were able to compete with free, tax-supported public schools. Some disbanded; others were absorbed into the public system; a few emerged as colleges, and still others changed their character by becoming exclusive college preparatory schools for the children of the wealthy.

It was not until the last quarter of the nineteenth century that public high schools became a firmly established part of the American educational scene. However, the beginnings of the movement occurred well before the Civil War. As might be expected the lead was taken by those states that had been among the first to lay down a system of common schools. Within all states development in cities preceded rural districts for a number of reasons. For one thing, they had the concentrated population from which to draw commuting students and the tax wealth with which to support free secondary schools. The variety of job opportunities available in cities and the skills they demanded seemed to call for more extensive preparation than the relatively simple tasks of the farm. Reformers pointed out that urban youth had more time available than did their country counterparts, thus leaving them free to be enticed into the kinds of unhealthy behavior the cities were prone to encourage. As a consequence, proponents of the high school argued, the moral lessons of the school were no less essential for impressionable adolescents than for their younger brothers and sisters in elementary grades.

Boston, which in the seventeenth century had established the first public Latin grammar school, inaugurated the high-school movement with the opening in 1821 of the English Classical School—later named the Boston English High School. In calling for community support the Boston school committee made it evident that they wished to found a public school alternative to the academy:

A parent who wishes to give a child an education that shall fit him for active life, and shall serve as a foundation for eminence in his profession, whether Mercantile or Mechanical, is under the necessity of giving him a different education from any which our public schools can now furnish. Hence, many children are separated from their parents and sent to private academies in this vicinity, to acquire that instruction which cannot be obtained at the public seminaries. Thus, many parents, who

*contribute largely to the support of these institutions, are sub-
ject to heavy expense for the same object in other towns.*

With the public Latin grammar school preparing students for
college entrance, there was no call for other than a terminal
education at the new institution. A student entered Boston English at the age of 12 and began a three-year course of study
including English composition and literature, declamation,
mathematics, natural science, history, ethics, and logic—very
much the pattern of the English tracks of many academies.
Then, as now, Boston English was a boys' school. The city's
commitment to secondary education for girls was not particularly firm at this time. A girls' high school, established in 1829,
was judged too expensive a project and was disbanded after
two years. Not until 1855 did Boston provide high school education for girls on a permanent basis. The mill town of Lowell,
Massachusetts earned the distinction of providing the first
model of the American comprehensive high school. In 1831 that
city established a coeducational high school offering both English and classical courses of study. Philadelphia's first high
school opened to boys and girls in 1838 with three tracks available: a classical curriculum of four years, a modern language
curriculum of four years, and a two-year English program.

Throughout the 1830s, 1840s, and 1850s the high-school movement slowly expanded. Smaller towns, lacking financial and
population resources, sometimes established a union school, an
institution offering both elementary and secondary education
under one roof. In larger population centers separate high
schools, generally providing at least two curriculum tracks,
were the rule, among them Baltimore (1839), Charleston (1840),
Providence (1843), Cleveland and Columbus (1846), New York
(1847), St. Louis (1853), Chicago and San Francisco (1856), and
Detroit (1858). A number of states enacted legislation permitting the utilization of tax funds to support public secondary
education. Massachusetts was unique in mandating in 1827 that
communities of 500 families or more furnish secondary level

courses in United States history, bookkeeping, geometry, surveying, and algebra, and that towns of 4000 or more families provide, in addition, college preparatory subjects, including Latin, Greek, history, rhetoric, and logic.

However, descriptions of high-school legislation and the listing of cities that provided secondary school facilities can be misleading. It cannot be emphasized too strongly that the high-school movement was in its infancy at this time. By 1860 there were approximately 300 high schools in the nation, over 100 located in Massachusetts alone. Compared with the more than 6000 academies, this represented a rather small drop in the secondary-school bucket. The disparity in numbers between the two kinds of schools can be partially explained by the fact that, as noted previously, the high school was basically an urban-oriented institution, dependent on tax support and commuting students. Despite the rapid growth of cities, America's population was still overwhelmingly rural. Yet, the gap was greater than it would have been if the high schools had been universally accepted by the populace of the nation's cities and towns. This clearly was not the case. In Massachusetts, for example, in spite of laws passed in 1827 and 1857 requiring secondary school offerings, several towns adamantly refused to establish high schools. At the close of the Civil War nearly 40 communities were legally delinquent in this matter.

Michael Katz in his brilliant study of school reform in Massachusetts (*The Irony of Early School Reform*, Cambridge, Mass., 1968) makes it quite clear that the high school was not an institution demanded by the masses. Instead, it was promoted by prosperous civic leaders in the name of social unity, community prosperity, and individual opportunity. In the high-school movement we find exemplified a kind of response to urbanization and industrialization typical of American reform from the Jacksonian era well into the twentieth century. Looking at the growth of the city, the solid citizen saw not only future wealth and prosperity but also signs of moral decay, class divisiveness, and challenges to the stability of church and family. With familiar reformer's optimism he turned to a progressive institution, the public school, to foster the good and check the evil, or, as Katz puts it, to "help build modern industrial cities permeated by the values and features of an idealized, rural life."

The response of members of the working class ranged, at different times in different towns, from lethargic acquiescence to active opposition. With the ballot in their hands the fate of the high school often depended on at which end of the spectrum their mood lay. An article in the Norwich, Connecticut *Weekly Courier* of November 25, 1856 made this point quite effectively:

... the studies of the high school, Algebra, Geometry, Chemistry, Natural Philosophy, Ancient History, Latin, Greek, French and German, were a perfect "terra incognita" to the great mass of the people. While the High School was a new thing and while a few enlightened citizens had control of it, in numerous instances it was carried to a high state of perfection. But after a time the burden of taxation would begin to be felt. Men would discuss the high salaries paid to the accomplished teachers which such schools demanded, and would ask, "To what purpose is this waste?" Demagogues, keen scented as wolves, would sniff the prey. "What do we want of a High School to teach rich men's children?" they would shout.

This statement supports Katz's findings that, despite reformers' insistence that they were democratizing secondary education, the very content of that education was judged by many to be fit only for "rich men's children." However, his investigations of school registers in Massachusetts indicate that the high school's appeal was actually greatest not among the extremely wealthy but among sons of middle-class farmers, artisans, and small businessmen who saw in the institution "a means of status maintenance and an entry into the business world . . . at a time when mechanization and other economic alterations made the future of their fathers' occupations less secure."

Even among the middle class, however, the high school, like the academy, attracted a minority of the youth. Whereas the expanded curriculum might appear more relevant than the old Latin grammar-school regimen, it still did not furnish preparation for specific trades or professions. Despite the assertion of reformers that they were offering education for life, as long as on-the-job training was available, most boys avoided formal education beyond the common school. This situation would ultimately change with the industrial and scientific explosions of the post-Civil War era. When factories came to employ thousands of workers, when the knowledge required to master technology, law, medicine, and business increased one hundred fold, the apprentice system proved unfeasible. Then leaders of industry and the professions allied themselves with reformers to successfully promote the high school. Until that day, many Americans considered learning beyond the rudiments as useless or a status symbol, as one of the fruits of the good life rather than a necessary step in attaining it.

Before leaving our discussion of secondary education, it is essential to examine the views and activities of still another sector of society, one that found neither the academies nor the high school satisfactory to its interests or the interests of the nation. Among representatives of America's most distinguished families were those who expressed considerable unhappiness over many of the trends of the Jacksonian period. These were the heirs of men who in the seventeenth and eighteenth centuries had achieved esteem through their services to colony, state, and nation and usually a measure of wealth through such means as trade, the professions, and land speculation and development. Socially and politically conservative in the Federalist tradition, many among them had no love for the democracy evolving in their midst. Nor did the newly enriched masters of industry and the industrial-urban society they were creating find favor in their eyes. In the Middle Atlantic States and the South most of them adhered to the Episcopal faith of their fathers. In New England too, the Episcopal was fast becoming the status church, winning through conversion or convenience several whose roots had been Congregationalist and whose previous worship had been Unitarian. Whatever their sect or commitment to it, however, they shared a general repugnance toward the popular evangelical movements of the day.

Despite their misgivings, these men in many respects shared the reformers' general optimism regarding the perfectibility of man and society and particular faith in the power of education to achieve this goal. Where they parted from the Manns and Barnards was in their concern with the education not of the masses but of the elite: their own sons and those of the new industrial capitalists. They had few doubts that talent and wealth would attain power, even in a democracy. What they wished to ensure was that this power would be wielded intelligently for socially useful ends by morally acceptable means. In short, they hoped for a nation governed by Christian scholars and gentlemen, and they labored to establish institutions through which to mold them. The resultant product was America's exclusive boarding schools.

The founding in 1855 of St. Paul's School in Concord, New Hampshire marked the culmination of their efforts during the antebellum period. The school's chief benefactor, Dr. George Cheyne Shattuck, explained his intentions:

We are desirous of endowing a school of the highest class, for boys, in which they may obtain an education which shall fit them either for college or business; including thorough intellectual training in the various branches of learning; gymnastic and manly exercises adapted to preserve health and strengthen the physical condition; such aesthetic culture and accomplishments as shall tend to refine the manners and elevate the taste, together with careful moral and religious instruction.

In the words of James McLachlan, St. Paul's "became the most influential model—accepted, rejected, but impossible to ignore—for the scores of private boarding schools founded in the decades after the Civil War." As McLachlan illustrates in his *American Boarding Schools: A Historical Study* (New York, 1970), St. Paul's itself was greatly influenced by the philosophies and practices of some of its short-lived predecessor institutions. Dr. Shattuck was an alumnus of Round Hill School, first of the boarding schools (1823–1834). The faculty was staffed with graduates of the pioneering Flushing Institute (1828-c. 1846), which like St. Paul's was affiliated with the Episcopal church. However, the origins of America's boarding schools go back farther than these early institutions. Both Round Hill and Flushing Institute had modeled themselves to a considerable extent on the secondary schools of Prussia and Switzerland, particularly on Fellenberg's school at Hofwyl.

Fellenberg's institution consisted of two parts, a farm and trade school for the peasantry and an academy for the upper classes. It was the latter that particularly attracted the founders of the American boarding school. There children were exposed to Fellenberg's conception of a total education, which stressed the development of the body and moral character as no less important than intellectual training. At Hofwyl the curriculum was expanded beyond the classical languages and mathematics to include natural science, modern languages, drawing, sculpting, and vocal and instrumental music. Portions of each day were devoted to games and nature hikes. Teaching methods stressed the use of the senses and at the same time denigrated rote memorization. Reward and punishment were discouraged as motivations for learning and correct behavior. In their place the role of the teacher was greatly expanded to that of an ever-present father figure who, by example and loving attention in a familylike setting, helped students achieve the goals of academic success, physical health, and virtuous character.

Not all of Fellenberg's innovations were successfully adopted by his American admirers. For example, they never did achieve the total elimination of reward and punishment. But they did extensively embrace the Swiss master's emphasis on the redeeming powers of nature, total or rounded education, and the school as an extension of the family. It was in the attainment of the latter objective that the advocates of the boarding school found the academies most lacking. Students boarding with private families in town, in addition to being exposed to unhealthy distractions of urban life, were denied the company of their classmates and the constant care and influence of their tutors. Following Fellenberg's lead, the fathers of the American boarding schools designed campuses for living as well as learning and set them in the midst of rural grandeur. To round out this ideal environment they firmly implanted the guiding hand of religion. The leaders of this movement shared none of Horace Mann's enthusiasm for nonsectarian religion. Flushing Institute, St. Paul's, and most subsequent boarding schools had definite ties with organized religions, the Episcopal predominating by far.

So it was in the great age of democracy, in the midst of a reform movement that would ultimately lead to the establishment of comprehensive public high schools as the predominant form of secondary education, that the boarding school, an elitist institution, was born. To this day it plays an important role in educating the children of some of the nation's most prominent families. In doing so, along with other forms of private and parochial schooling, it has prevented the public schools from embracing all the children of the community and from receiving the fullest support of all citizens.

There is a note of irony in the fact that the example of Fellenberg's school inspired both the founders of exclusive boarding schools and the radical reformer Robert Dale Owen. It is no less ironical that, during the same era in which Round Hill, Flushing Institute, and St. Paul's were established, there appeared an institution founded upon quite similar principles but designed for a totally different clientele. On December 8, 1848 the first state reform school was opened at Westborough, Massachusetts. By 1860 there were over 100 around the country. Like the advocates of boarding schools, penal reformers were

keenly alert to the adverse influences of the city and ameliora-
tive qualities of a rural institutional setting. Similar to boarding schools, reform schools were designed to provide a morally
superior environment, complete with a program of constant,
constructive activity and a form of social organization pat-
terned after the family. In this case the choice was female
teachers acting as mother figures. As McLachlan reminds us,
the reform schools, unlike the elite boarding schools, were
meant "not to educate Christian gentlemen and scholars but
frugal and industrious workers." The success of the boarding
schools in achieving their objectives might be subject to some
conjecture. Unfortunately, there exists sufficient evidence to
indicate that reform schools have often been more successful
in breeding adult criminals than responsible citizen-workers.

Of all the levels of schooling, none so thoroughly represents
a break with tradition and acceptance of the scientific and
idealistic outlook that had its origins in the writings of Locke
and Rousseau as does the kindergarten. The father of the kindergarten movement was Friedrich Froebel (1782–1852), a
German who had been greatly influenced by his experiences as
a teacher at Pestalozzi's school at Yverdon and by the romantic
idealism of the post-Kantian movement in philosophy. Froebel
believed that the ultimate purpose of education "is the realization of a faithful, pure, inviolate, and therefore holy life." It
was the school's responsibility, he wrote, to "develop the divine
spirit in man and make him conscious of it, so that his life may
become a free expression of that spirit. Education, in other
words, should lead man to a clear knowledge of himself, to
peace with nature, to unity with God." He strongly argued that
this process begin in early childhood, even before the child was
ready to be exposed to the traditional rudiments. Just as the
older child learns through reading, the child of three and four,
Froebel insisted, acquires knowledge in a natural way through
playing games and manipulating objects, to many of which he
assigned symbolic and "useful" values. The ball, for example,
he viewed not only as a plaything but as a teacher of numerous

concepts of physics and a symbol of the unity of the world. In the child's garden—the kindergarten—adults would provide the setting and objects of educational value, but the child would be allowed to freely express himself with minimal interference: ". . . the fundamental principles of education, instruction, and teaching, should be passive and protective, not directive and interfering."

While the kindergarten movement spread throughout Germany and then through the rest of Western Europe prior to mid-century, it was virtually unknown in the United States. Educational leaders here were preoccupied with expanding and improving traditional forms of schooling. Even if this had not been the case, it is difficult to imagine pragmatic Americans of this era favorably responding to the romantic, mystical idealism which surrounded Froebel's school. We had moved a considerable distance from the Puritan view of a harsh God, sinful man, and even more sin-prone children, but not this far. When one contemplates the opposition to Mann's advocacy of new methods and more lenient discipline, support for a school in which play and enjoyment were the only observable results seems inconceivable. Even stripped of its Froebellian mysticism, not until the end of the nineteenth century would the kindergarten be widely accepted ·as the first rung on our educational ladder.

Nevertheless, beginning in 1855 a handful of kindergartens did appear in the United States, all but one founded by German refugees from the upheavals of 1848. The first was organized by Mrs. Carl Schurz in Watertown, Wisconsin. Prior to 1865 others, usually affiliated with private German-English academies, appeared in Columbus, Ohio; Hoboken, New Jersey; New York City; Newton, Massachusetts; Louisville, Kentucky, and Boston. The larger American community probably first learned of the kindergarten in 1856 through the pages of Henry Barnard's *American Journal of Education*. Barnard had visited an English kindergarten in 1854 while serving as a delegate to the International Exhibit of Educational Systems and Materials. In 1859 two American travellers described the kindergartens of Germany and outlined Froebel's principles in an article appearing in the *Christian Examiner*. These pieces aroused the interest of Horace Mann's sister-in-law, Elizabeth Palmer Peabody. Her participation in the romantic Transcendentalist movement apparently made her more receptive to Froebel's philosophy than most of her hardnosed countrymen. A chance meeting with Mrs. Schurz in the winter of 1859 was all that was needed to transform curiosity into action. The following year she opened a kindergarten in Boston. However, a sense of her own inadequacy led her to abandon the project after a few years and set sail for Europe to observe kindergartens and study Froebel's ideas. Upon returning she devoted considerable energy to promoting the kindergarten by means of lectures and writing.

There was a further development in the closing years of the period that played a significant role in winning converts not only for the kindergarten but for the broader "new education" movement inaugurated by Pestalozzi. In 1861 Dr. Edward A. Sheldon, superintendent of schools in Oswego, New York, established a department for training the city's teachers on Pestalozzian principles. Sheldon's work was so successful that in 1863 the department was expanded to become the Oswego Normal School. There students became acquainted with the latest findings regarding child development and the need to relate teaching to children's interests and capacities. They were fully indoctrinated in the philosophy of freedom and self-expression in education and instructed in the techniques of the Pestalozzian object lessons. Oswego emerged as the leading normal school of the day, and its graduates were highly sought after by superintendents and principals throughout the nation. Through them the teachings of Pestalozzi as interpreted by Sheldon received a wide and often enthusiastic hearing.

One of the most frequently cited indicators of the expansionist spirit of antebellum America is the phenomenal growth of colleges that occurred. Of the approximately 250 colleges in existence at the time of the firing on Fort Sumter, 182 still survive. Of the latter, 133 had been founded during the previous three decades. Remarkable as these figures are, they tell only part of the story. Over 500 colleges had been established in the years between the Revolutionary and Civil Wars and had subsequently failed. Fire, disease, insufficient funds, a potential market that never materialized—these and other vicissitudes of frontier America constituted the rocks upon which many a young institution foundered.

The obvious parallels between the creation of colleges and of new businesses extend beyond the domain of risks involved. The competitive spirit was also very much a part of the college movement. One observer noted in 1858, "Each denomination seems anxious to outdo the other in the number of Colleges and Schools. This spirit of rivalry has proved itself contagious, as well as debilitating." Of 182 colleges that endured, 104 had been founded with religious support and affiliation. The Presbyterians led with 32, closely followed by the Methodists, Baptists, Congregationalists, and Catholics with some 15 other sects trailing behind.

While each denomination was determined to install its particular brand of Christianity and to educate future ministers of their faith, they were not so callous as to restrict their student bodies to children of their own congregants. Nor, in stating their objectives, were they neglectful of an obligation to enhance the welfare of state and nation. Colleges would train Christian gentlemen, examples to all not only of piety but also of industriousness, loyalty, and a high moral character. Society at large, it was promised, would benefit immensely by its support of these institutions. Assurances were given that democracy would be advanced, for the new denominational colleges, no less than the state universities, would delve deeply into all strata of society in their search for virtuous and talented youth.

Very much a part of the spirit of expanding educational opportunity on all levels was an accompanying climate of nonintellectualism. Among most colleges, fostering piety and virtue took precedence over developing appreciation and love of learning. The newer institutions, however, terribly deficient in scholarly resources, embraced this position with particular fervor. Chapel and dormitory were judged of no less importance in the education of Christian gentlemen than the classroom. Faculty, standing *in loco parentis*, were often honored more for their moral influence than their academic credentials. Learning was valued neither for its own sake nor for any immediately practical purposes.

By the 1840s a few particularly well endowed and staffed institutions offered their students elementary courses in physics, astronomy, chemistry, and even modern languages. But these were generally considered studies of relatively low status, certainly not worthy of replacing or being offered as alternatives to the major courses. Tradition, supported by the influential Yale Report of 1828 (published in 1829), dictated a curriculum dominated by classical languages and literature with their handmaidens mathematics, logic, and moral philosophy. Classroom procedures were restricted almost totally to faculty lectures and to student recitations of memorized lessons. In the words of President Jeremiah Day of Yale, "The two great points to be gained in intellectual culture are the *discipline* and the *furniture* of the mind; expanding the powers and storing it with knowledge. The former of these is, perhaps, the more important of the two."

The Yale Report was the most authoritative document in the area of higher education during the decades preceding the Civil War. The smallest colleges in the most-isolated spots of the West with the most meagerly prepared students and inadequately trained faculty took Yale's curriculum as their guide. The results were often ludicrous. Though they adhered to the democratic spirit of the day in welcoming matriculants from all levels of society, they had little of practical value to attract the young man eager to get ahead in a nation on the edge of frontiers in science, technology, business, and government. Despite the numerical growth of colleges during these years, the proportion of college graduates steadily declined.

Many of those who did attend the colleges apparently set their hopes on the potential power and prestige of the B.A. degree. Certainly the social snobbishness that generally characterized student clubs leads one to suspect that their members were not particularly sensitive to charges of aristocratic pomposity being leveled at the colleges. Yet, they, too, were far from pleased with conditions on campus. They objected to the drab, cold environment of the dormitory, the restrictions placed on behavior and movement, and the greater attention to saving the soul than to developing the mind. The antebellum college might have been a fine place for ministers-to-be, but fewer and fewer graduates sought this vocation—from approximately 30 percent in 1836 to 20 percent in 1861. In contrast, beginning in the 1840s there was a sharp rise in the percentage of college graduates entering into business careers.

Frustrated by what they found lacking in the environment and studies provided for them, students took it upon themselves to fill the void through their own organizations. Student literary and debating societies established libraries, which often surpassed the colleges' collections not only in terms of numbers of volumes but also in the kinds of literature available. The latest works in science, politics, fiction, and history filled their shelves. The outside world was brought to the campus through leading personalities from several walks of life, who accepted invitations from the societies to deliver addresses. Other contributions to the intellectual life of the colleges by these organizations included student debates on contemporary social and political issues, the publication of literary journals, and the founding of natural history museums.

During the 1840s and 1850s the Greek letter fraternities began to spread among the colleges. By 1870 they had virtually replaced the literary societies as the major form of student organization. Although the fraternities initially duplicated many of the intellectual activities of the older associations, as historian Frederick Rudolph points out, they were primarily organized "to fill an emotional rather than a curriculum vacuum." They provided both a substitute for the family the students had left behind and an escape from the lack of privacy and oppressive moral atmosphere of the college. No doubt the secret rituals and social activities of fraternities presented heavy competition for the serious-minded literary and debating societies. However, the rise of the former and decline of the latter were the results of more than a substitution of interests among students. Beginning in the post-Civil War years curriculum reform progressed at a fairly rapid rate, and colleges provided many of the studies and facilities once available only through student organizations. A similar movement from student to institutional sponsorship occurred in the area of organized games and gymnastics.

Turning to administrators and faculty, despite general acceptance among them of the philosophy of the Yale Report, there were those who carried on the tradition of George Ticknor of Harvard in attempting to reform higher education, to make it more intellectually respectable and relevant to the needs of society. Francis Wayland, president of Brown University, after many years of pleading finally elicited from the trustees permission to attempt significant changes at the college. He wanted students to be given opportunities to elect the courses they desired; he advocated the abandonment of the rigid, semester-length course system and its replacement with a variable time approach based upon the value and difficulty of the particular subject; he urged the creation of programs in agriculture, applied science, law, and pedagogy, and the awarding of the Ph.B. and M.A. degrees as well as the traditional B.A.

In 1851, with his proposals applauded not only in reform-minded academic circles but also by journalists and political and industrial leaders, Wayland launched his experiment. Unfortunately, within five years the new direction was reversed and Wayland replaced as president. A majority on the Brown faculty found it impossible to adjust to the freedom and flexibility implicit in the new approach. They viewed with contempt the candidates for the less-demanding Ph.B. degree. Furthermore, the school lacked the finances and sizable student body with which to support the extended curriculum and specialized fields Wayland had proposed.

Among reformers in higher education, Francis Wayland was by no means unique in having experienced failure. One of his most noteworthy colleagues was Henry Tappan, who as president of the University of Michigan unsuccessfully attempted to bring scholarly graduate education on the German model to a state barely emerged from its pioneer beginnings and mistrustful of foreign ideas and intellectual ideals. However, though Brown and the University of Michigan returned to the traditional methods of educating Christian gentlemen, and Wayland and Tappan joined the ranks of reformers whom history records as being in advance of their times, their experiments did, in fact, help herald the approach of an era of widespread reform in collegiate education.

Even by the 1850s and 1860s American higher education was beginning to offer alternatives to the classical curriculum to youths willing to forego the B.A. for the lower status but more practical programs leading to a B.S. or Ph.B. At midcentury Rensselaer Polytechnic Institute (founded in 1824) was flourishing, offering extensive degree programs in the natural sciences and engineering. The school employed scientific field work, visits to mines and factories, and teaching laboratories, all pioneering teaching techniques designed to stress the practical applications of learning. The list of independent technical schools grew with the founding of Brooklyn Polytechnic Institute (1854), Cooper Union (1859), and the Massachusetts Institute of Technology (1865). The age of science and technology had arrived, and even conservative Yale could not ignore that fact. In 1847 Yale established new chairs in agriculture and in chemistry and applied science that became the nucleus from which the Sheffield Scientific School emerged. Endowments from industrialists help launch the Lawrence Scientific School at Harvard (1848) and Dartmouth's Chandler School of Science (1851). In 1855 legislative action inaugurated the first state agricultural colleges in Michigan and Pennsylvania. Finally, as an alternative to the separate school approach to modern studies, a handful of colleges offered scientific and literary programs. Students electing to follow this track were provided three-year concentrations in the natural sciences and modern languages as contrasted with the heavy emphasis on classical languages and philosophy of the traditional, four year, B.A. curriculum.

As one examines the history of higher education during this period, it becomes apparent that one or more of the assets of wealth, prestige, and political skill were often significant in transforming visions of institutional reform into reality. From commerce and industry came the contributions of the Peter Coopers, Lawrences, Sheffields, and Van Rensselaers. From the political arena came Justin Morrill, Whig congressman from Vermont, who with consummate skill guided the passage of an act whose provisions ensured a permanent place for collegiate level agricultural and engineering studies. Under the provisions of the Morrill Act of 1862 millions of acres of federal lands were apportioned among the states on the basis of 30,000 acres for each member of the Senate and House of Representatives. Proceeds from the sale of the land were earmarked explicitly for the support in each state of at least one school "where the leading object shall be, without excluding other scientific or classical studies, to teach such branches of learning as are related to agriculture and the mechanic arts."

One surmises that most of the congressmen who voted for Morrill's bill did not have the slightest idea that they were taking sides in a long-standing debate over the nature and function of higher education. They had responded to arguments appealing to a broad base of interests. Morrill employed statistics to emphasize the steady decline in yield-per-acre of farm land. The nation's mechanics were described as having both a great desire and need for higher education. Congress was assured that the land grant colleges would benefit not only those who attended but the population at large, because these institutions would experiment in new techniques in agriculture and technology and disseminate their findings widely. Farmers' sons, educated in scientific agriculture, would be less likely to leave for the cities. Morrill cleverly appealed to national pride by pointing out that Europe was well ahead of the United States in governmental assistance to agriculture. Russia in particular, that "growing giant of Europe," he warned, was taking a "conspicuous lead" in education and was second only to France in the number of its agricultural schools. How could our enlightened republic permit the land of the despotic czars to get the jump on us? Besides, the bill provided an equitable and sensible way of distributing federal lands among the states.

Today, nearly 70 institutions are benefactors of the Morrill Act and subsequent supportive legislation. Some are A and M (agricultural and mechanical) colleges that were founded specifically in response to the act; some are land grant-supported schools or colleges, component parts of large state universities; others are found on the campuses of otherwise private universities.

There was still another area of higher education that felt the winds of reform during these years. Liberal thought regarding the status of women, together with an emergent women's rights movement, not unnaturally led to demands for broader educational and professional opportunities. Women educational leaders of a moderate stamp joined Horace Mann and Henry Barnard in applauding the feminizing of the teaching profession. These reformers believed that the motherly instinct of female teachers would constitute a powerful force for checking the passions of men, which threatened to turn class against class, section against section. It was this certainty that women could and should be educated to be more than fancy adornments in a male world that motivated leaders like Catherine Beecher, Emma Willard, and Mary Lyons. While they viewed teaching as an excellent occupation for the unmarried, their ultimate interest was to prepare women to function more effectively in their natural and noble roles of wives and mothers. In the words of Mary Lyon, founder of Mount Holyoke Female Seminary, "O how immensely important is this work of preparing the daughters of the land to be good mothers!"

What these women sought to achieve at schools like Hartford Female Seminary (Beecher), Troy Female Seminary (Willard), and Mount Holyoke was to provide their students with more than the traditional polite studies of art, music, drawing, and modern languages. Convinced that women were particularly endowed with the capacity to spread God's word, they took care to ensure that the climate and teachings of their institutions would foster good Christian character. The role of keeper of the home, having been declared both a worthy and demanding one, required no less attention than the development of the mind. Indeed, as Miss Beecher pointed out, "a problem in arithmetic or geometry is far more interesting, and therefore more quickening to the intellect, when it is directly applied to some useful purpose." And so the young ladies were trained to do well what, in the opinion of these educational leaders, they were particularly equipped to do. They studied history, geography, science, and literature to make them informed and interesting companions to their husbands and effective teachers of children, physical training and the domestic sciences to ensure a healthy family and well-ordered home, and religious training so that they and those whom they influenced would be guided by the spirit of God.

When compared with today's leaders of the women's liberation movement and even with the more radical female activists of their own day like Frances Wright, Lucretia Mott, and Susan B. Anthony, the early directors of women's education appear rather tame. They did not seek for their sex equality of rights and opportunities. Their schools, although often designated colleges, were hardly comparable to the traditional B.A.-granting institutions for men. Catherine Beecher frankly stated in 1851 that "not one" female seminary calling itself a college had "as yet, secured the chief advantages of such institutions. They are merely high schools." Nevertheless, Miss Beecher and her colleagues are truly deserving of the title "pioneers." By insisting that women were capable of receiving an education beyond the rudiments, by proclaiming the superiority of their sex as teachers of the young, and by stressing the crucial roles of motherhood they were challenging not only prevailing masculine attitudes but also those held by a majority of women. At the beginning of the era, in 1830, women were everywhere figuratively in chains. Law and tradition denied them rights in virtually all spheres of life. When women began entering the mills and came to dominate the common-school teaching corps, a most significant breech in the wall of sexual *status quo* occurred. Reforms among the female seminaries represented attempts to take immediate advantage of the initial currents of change. The cause of women's rights, the struggle for complete social, political, economic, and educational equality—a longer, more hazardous enterprise—was left for others.

The women's-rights movement could point to some impressive gains by 1865. Beginning with Mississippi in 1839, eight states had granted wives the right to control their own property. In 1860 New York granted mothers joint guardianship over their children. The Congregationalist Church broke new ground in 1852 when it ordained Mrs. Antoinette Louisa Brown Blackwell. In education the cause of sexual equality was advanced when Oberlin College inaugurated coeducation in 1838, offering its female students a choice of a ladies' course or the traditional curriculum. In 1842 four young women received Bachelor of Arts degrees from that Ohio institution. As one Oberlin student put it, "Women are to be educated because we choose civilization rather than barbarism." Antioch in 1853 and the University of Iowa in 1860 also chose "civilization," and in 1859 Elmira Female College in New York became the first women's college to award its students an honest-to-goodness B.A. degree. Ten years earlier at another upstate New York institution, the Geneva Medical College, Elizabeth Blackwell had become the first American woman to receive a medical degree. Incidentally, she graduated first in her class.

Despite some victories, however, the war was hardly won by the feminists during these years. Only the benefit of hindsight informs us that these were the first of many successes that were to come later, sometimes many years later. In 1865 the better medical and theological schools were firmly shut to women; the opportunities for women to receive a collegiate education were extremely limited. What today's feminists call "male chauvinism" was solidly entrenched in the land. Even within reform circles women sometimes had to struggle to gain participation as equals. In 1840 at the World Anti-Slavery Convention at London female delegates from the United States were denied access to the podium and were obliged to observe the proceedings from behind a screen in the balcony. In this country the National Teachers Association withheld equal membership status for women until 1866.

What we see occurring in the area of higher education during this period in many ways duplicates events in several other spheres of American life: a call for reform in more democratic and utilitarian directions often effectively impeded by a conservative establishment. The needs for an expanded collegiate curriculum, for an elective course system, for professional and technical education, and for quality education for women were dramatically articulated by a group of outstanding educational reformers, but in large measure the spirit of the Yale Report ruled the day.

Ideally, the nature of competitive enterprise dictates that when one firm fails to provide the customer the services he desires, another will surely arise to do the job. In a sense this principle has often applied to the field of education. Today encyclopedias, great books collections, educational toys, adult-education classes, and correspondence courses are offered to the public as supplements to or to fill the gaps of formal schooling. The failure of traditional institutions of pre-Civil War America to respond to popular educational needs was, to no small extent, offset by the spread of the lyceum movement and the rise of public libraries. The enthusiasm with which they were greeted by the middle-class public is indicative of the hunger for knowledge beyond that available in the schools.

The American Lyceum movement was the inspiration of Josiah Holbrook, a Connecticut farmer, scholar, and educator who had earned part of his livelihood by delivering lectures on geology to adult groups around the state. In 1826 he proposed in Barnard's *American Journal of Education* a federation of adult educational organizations, called "lyceums," on town, county, state, and national levels. That same year he assisted in the establishment of the first town lyceum in Millbury, Massachusetts. From then on the movement spread rapidly, particularly through New England, New York, Pennsylvania, and the Midwest. By 1828 there were over 100 town lyceums; three years later delegates representing 1000 town lyceums met in New York City to organize the National American Lyceum. In 1835 Holbrook estimated the existence of 15 or 16 state lyceums, over 100 county lyceums, and approximately 3000 town and village lyceums.

The elaborate hierarchical plan of organization envisioned by Holbrook never really materialized. Attendance at the national conventions decreased yearly until the final meeting in 1839. However, on the local level the lyceums continued to flourish through the Civil War years. Holbrook had defined the town lyceum as "a voluntary association of individuals [men and women] disposed to improve each other in useful knowledge and to advance the interests of the schools." He described how in their early years they accomplished the first objective:

... *they hold weekly or other stated meetings, for reading, conversation, discussion, illustrating the sciences, or other exercises designed for their mutual benefit; and as it is found convenient, they collect a cabinet, consisting of apparatus for illustrating the sciences, books, minerals, plants, or other natural or artificial productions.*

In addition, Holbrook reported that many lyceum groups engaged in the organization of libraries and the compilation of town histories, town maps, and agricultural and geological surveys. Holbrook's great personal interest was the advancement of scientific knowledge, and a good deal of the "apparatus" he wrote of was of his own design and manufacture. However, the topics for discussion went beyond science to embrace most of the issues and interests of the day, including education, literature, the advancement of industry and technology, tariffs, and internal improvements. Only war and slavery were initially discouraged as subjects too controversial for inclusion. Yet, as the Civil War approached it became impossible to exclude them.

Through their programs to promote and serve the public schools the lyceums acted as invaluable allies of the reform leaders. The endeavor became the common project of all lyceums, and they did more than provide a forum for its espousal. Holbrook reported that they often furnished "teachers with a room, apparatus, and other accommodations, for holding meetings, and conducting a course of exercises in relation to their schools. . . ." They encouraged the attendance of older children at various lyceum sessions, conscious of the value of expanding their knowledge beyond the limitations of the local school's curriculum.

As might be expected, after a number of years of listening to debates and discussions by homebred talent, the lyceums sought to bring speakers from the outside. Leaders in several fields welcomed the opportunity to present their views and talents before audiences eager to hear them, and what amounted to a national lyceum circuit emerged. The fascinating wonders of science were detailed by men such as Benjamin Silliman of Yale and Louis Agassiz of Harvard; advocates of numerous reform causes appeared as lecturers. To their credit the lyceums sought out not only moderate reformers like Henry Barnard and Horace Mann, but eventually also leaders of more controversial movements, including women's rights (Susan B. Anthony) and abolition (William Lloyd Garrison and Wendell Phillips). One can imagine the excitement in town when literary figures whose works had occupied numerous discussion sessions came to address the local lyceum. Among them were Thoreau, Holmes, Dickens, Thackeray, and, most popular of all, Ralph Waldo Emerson.

The interests and activities of the lyceums represented so much of what Americans desired from the storehouse of knowledge: not knowledge for its own sake or as a status symbol but, instead, learning that was useful and a source of enjoyment as well. In the spirit of Benjamin Franklin, they shunned the existing institutions of higher learning for their irrelevance and with utmost faith turned to self-culture. It is no wonder that one of the most sought-after lecturers was Elihu Burritt, "the learned blacksmith," who in displaying mastery of nearly 50 languages proved both entertaining and the epitome of the self-educated man.

Still another avenue to self-culture—a more subdued and individualistic one for the learner—was provided by the libraries, which arose in large numbers during these years. There were several varieties already existent by 1830: mechanics' and apprentices' libraries, subscription libraries, lyceum libraries, and mercantile libraries. All were quasi-private, supported by membership fees or the donations of institutional or private benefactors. Of greater long-run significance, however, were the free, public libraries that appeared in the years ahead. During the 1830s and 1840s a few New England towns followed the lead of Peterborough, New Hampshire, which in 1833 had utilized municipal funds to support a free town library. There followed state laws specifically permitting towns to found and maintain tax-supported municipal libraries. New Hampshire was first with a statewide law in 1849, followed by Massachusetts in 1851, Maine in 1854, and Vermont in 1855. These provided the legal precedents for a movement that would eventually become national.

The public library movement, as with all the reform endeavors to which we have referred, cannot be fully understood outside the context of the era in which it was born—the fantastic decades before the Civil War. It was partly made possible by technical advances that enabled the written word to be reproduced more rapidly and at substantially lower cost than before. This applied not only to books but also to an increasing quantity and variety of newspapers and magazines. It was also most certainly a response to a population that, owing to the common schools, was more literate and—another effect of technology—more able to find leisure time for reading. The fact that the movement developed during America's first golden age of literature was probably more than mere coincidence. Finally, the public-library movement joined with other reform causes in proclaiming the era's seemingly limitless faith in man's ability through his institutions to improve himself and society. Recognizing this common outlook, it should come as no real surprise that, in his history of the public library (*Arsenals of a Democratic Culture*, Chicago, 1947), Sidney Ditzion identified as the leaders of the movement three men who are familiar for their roles in other areas of educational reform: Francis Wayland, Edward Everett, and George Ticknor.

Francis Wayland as early as 1838 urged the members of the Providence Athenaeum to open their collection to the public. Expressing a point of view similar to the one he later revealed as president of Brown, he argued that any citizen of Providence should be able to attain "all the reading which shall be necessary to prepare him for any situation for which his cultural endowments have rendered him capable."

Everett and Ticknor joined forces to labor in behalf of the founding of the Boston Public Library.[1] They both insisted that the institution contain a collection so comprehensive as to serve both the research needs of scholars and the practical needs of professionals, mechanics, artists, and artisans. Everett, who as governor of Massachusetts had allied himself closely with Horace Mann, was a particularly effective promoter of the concept of the library as a vehicle for continuing education

---

[1] In 1848 Massachusetts enacted legislation specifically permitting Boston to use public funds to support its projected library.

beyond the common-school years. However, it was George Ticknor who successfully lobbied for the adoption of practices that made the Boston Public Library unique in its time and a model for the future. His fellow planners had envisioned a reference library designed for adults. Ticknor urged that facilities be made available to school children as well. Even more important, he called for an institution:

which, in the main *department and purpose should differ from all free libraries yet attempted. I mean one in which any popular books, tending to moral and intellectual improvement, should be furnished in such numbers of copies that many persons, if they desired it, could be reading the same book at the same time; in short, that not only the best books of all sorts, but the pleasant literature of the day, should be made accessible to the whole people.*

Ticknor further recommended an open-shelves system, consultation services, and the privileges of circulation of popular works for home reading.

Time and again in his writings, George Ticknor revealed a solid faith in the abilities of the "mass of people" to improve themselves with the aid of institutions such as the common school and the public library. Unlike many reformers he seems to have been motivated less by fear of mobocracy and more by confidence in the potential of a society of educated citizens. Unlike so many intellectuals he did not condemn out-of-hand popular tastes and interests. Instead he saw the possibilities that these could "by a little judicious help, rather than by any direct control or restraint, be carried much higher than is generally thought possible." It was precisely this kind of outlook that governed the lyceum and library movements and gained for them a large measure of popular support. If those who led the colleges had been as astute, they might well have avoided the indifference and hostility that greeted them in an era when so many sought to learn.

chapter five
other places, other people

the common-school movement provides abundant evidence that a nation was emerging from among the several states that had cautiously agreed to form a political union. The so-called "Yankee device" ultimately became an American institution largely because men and ideas refused to be confined by the parochialisms of state or regional loyalties. Once the new territories of the West overcame being selfconscious about their rude frontier condition, they willingly embraced the trappings of what their Eastern cousins called civilized life. Reformers and schoolmarms, textbooks and journals traveled back and forth across the nation, leaving in their wake the little red schoolhouse, as American as apple pie. Glancing at Winslow Homer's charming painting of children playing in the field beside a one-room schoolhouse ["Snap the Whip" (1872)] one would find it impossible to determine, without the artist providing the information, in just what section of the nation the scene was set.

Yet it is common knowledge that there were exceptions to this rosy picture. By 1860 the states of the South had repudiated many ideals and modes that characterized the emerging nationalism and had chosen to follow their own separate and distinct path of economic, social, and political development. A Southern regionalism was the product of three decades that saw the section's leadership move from a position that tended to ignore or be apologetic for such conditions as slavery, a rigid class system, and a high rate of illiteracy to one that aggressively insisted that these would actually benefit the creation of a superior civilization. And the blacks, too, were major exceptions, exceptions without choice. Whether slave or freedman, whether residing in the North or South, the Negro was denied full participation in society. The history of education as it affected both Negroes and white Southerners provides a remarkable microcosm of the broad social history of these people during the antebellum period. It also enables us to examine the roots of contemporary educational practices as they apply to these two groups, practices that to this day make them, in many respects, exceptions to the rule.

Where tax-supported public schooling was concerned, the South in 1830 was not particularly unique. As in the rest of the nation, it was virtually nonexistent. The movement for school reform was in its infancy here also. However, despite these similarities, even at this early date there were differences perceivable that set the South apart from her sister states. As we noted in the first chapter, the traditions and conditions of Southern society from colonial times made its soil particularly poor for the flourishing of reform. At the outset of the nineteenth century no other section could duplicate the existence of a class so powerful as the planter aristocracy of the upper South. Conservative in general where property taxes were concerned, the most extreme wing held views toward public education not dissimilar from those stated by John Randolph of Roanoke at the Virginia Constitutional Convention of 1829–1830:

Look at that ragged fellow staggering from the whiskey shop, and see that slattern who has gone to reclaim him; where are

their children? Running about, ragged, idle, ignorant, fit candi-
dates for the penitentiary. Why is all this so? Ask the man and
he will tell you, "Oh, the Government has undertaken to edu-
cate our children for us. It has given us a premium for idle-
ness, and I now spend in liquor, what I should otherwise be
obliged to save to pay for their schooling."

To men of Randolph's persuasion education was clearly a
responsibility to be borne by parents. Publicly supported
schooling, they argued, not only resulted in an unfair infringement upon property but also interfered with the rights and
obligations of fathers. More charitable associates of Randolph
were willing to accept the notion of orphan and pauper education supported by a state literary fund fed by revenue from
fines and licenses. But beyond this they refused to go.

The political power of the upper South planters extended
further than their numbers in relation to the total population.
This was partly the result of property qualifications for voting
that were higher and remained longer in these states than in
the rest of the nation. Power also derived from the benefits of
plural voting that entitled a landowner to cast a ballot in each
county in which he owned property. Finally, control by the
planter aristocracy of the county courts was most significant.
These were the primary agencies of local government, run by
officers who were appointed rather than elected. It was through
them that the monies from the state school fund passed. Once
the needs of the paupers had been met, it was not unusual for
the balance of the money to be directed by the courts to the
support of local private academies. As Professor Welter points
out, the academies were sometimes further aided when children of the poor were enrolled at public expense.

Ironically, in the lower South, where the spirit of Jacksonian democracy was rampant and where suffrage was widely
distributed, the small farmers proved to be as adamant foes
of the common school as the planter aristocracy of Virginia

and the Carolinas. Here conditions and attitudes were not unlike those of the Western territories. Unfortunately, however, the rural South was pitifully slow in losing its frontier character. Few New England missionaries or schoolmarms ventured in this direction to challenge attitudes toward education that ranged from apathy to outright opposition. As Clement Eaton stresses, physical illness and a strong sense of pride among the poor whites of the South often contributed to shaping this negative stance. Generations passed before the debilitating effects of hookworm, malaria, and ague were fully appreciated and their causes checked. Also, as with their fellows throughout the nation, the poor of the South often viewed the required declarations of indigence with such repugnance that they chose to keep their children out of school.

Despite the particularly overwhelming odds against them, a group of dedicated school reform leaders did emerge in the Southland. A goodly number of them were Whigs, and in several instances they were men who had risen to positions of distinction in society from rather humble beginnings. Their arguments, not unlike those of their Northern colleagues, stressed the contributions common schools would make to morality, social harmony, and the preservation of republican institutions. The speech on behalf of common schooling delivered by Congressman Henry A. Wise of Virginia in 1844 could easily have been the creation of a Mann or a Barnard. He told his constituents, "There should be no distinction between children of a republic. They are not in the school sense the children of their parents, but the state is *parens patriae*, and they should all be regarded as sons and daughters of Mother Commonwealth."

In Tennessee Andrew Johnson battled western slaveholders in the cause of the common school. Georgia's governor, Joseph E. Brown, adding a Southern note to an otherwise familiar reform plea, called for a "Common School, not a Poor School System. Let there be no aristocracy there but an aristocracy of color and conduct." C. G. Memminger in aristocratic South Carolina argued that "the bringing together the children of the rich and the poor will benefit both, by removing from one any disposition to arrogance and self-will, and from the other the spirit of envy and jealousy." In Louisiana federal judge Theodore H. McCaleb in 1844 urged the state to advance a system of enlightened public education which would be an inspiration to the rest of the South and, beyond that, to the nation as a whole:

Yea, that the whole South, yielding to the influence of our own bright example, may soon cause the pure and limpid waters of social existence, which shall bountifully flow from the system we this day advocate, to roll back upon their great Northern source, until our whole happy Union . . . shall pour forth a perennial flood of moral intelligence.

Advocates of common schooling were few, but they were well placed, hopeful, even optimistic. They gained strength from the successes of Northern reformers, with whom they exchanged letters and from whom they sought advice and guidance. Sentiments like McCaleb's could still be applauded in the South of the 1840s. Southerners were very much involved in the Mexican War and took great satisfaction in the territorial expansion of the Union that resulted from that conflict and the settlement of the Oregon boundary dispute. It was not unreasonable to hope that the spirit of nationalism might yet embrace the several nationwide reform causes, including the common school.

But, of course, that was not to be. On the heels of territorial expansion followed the issue of the spread of slavery. The optimism and nationalism of the 1840s yielded to the bitter wranglings and growing divisiveness of the 1850s. Spokesmen for Southern separatism gained a larger audience as the years passed. Well before political secession they demanded cultural independence, arguing that Southern "life, habits, thoughts, and arms" were "so essentially different from those of the North." Some advocates, writing in *De Bow's Commercial*

Review and the *Southern Literary Messenger*, proposed that the schools could be useful instruments for achieving this end. Southern literature would be enriched and loyalty to Southern institutions would be assured, they insisted, when children were educated in their home districts by Southern-bred teachers instructing from textbooks prepared by Southern authors. Added to this was the argument that Northern schools, teachers, and texts were "fraught with peril to our sacred institutions." In 1856 the drive for cultural independence gained support at the Savannah Convention, where a committee of prominent professors was constituted to prepare school books with a Southern orientation.

As extreme as such sentiment might appear, there were many among the proslavery leadership whose views on schooling had moved even further to the right by the eve of the Civil War. In their minds mistrust of outside influences was eventually joined by suspicion of local institutions. Democratic principles were dispelled by conceptions of government and education as the exclusive domains of an aristocratic ruling class. Educating the poor and laboring classes, they insisted, would only arouse dissatisfaction with their lot. Social order would be endangered. As Rush Welter concluded, "In the final analysis the proslavery argument treated public education as a positive evil in American society."

A number of historians have compiled data from census reports and other sources that effectively depict the results of the neglect of popular education in the South. It is a sad picture. Census figures for 1850 show that the states of the South had an illiteracy ratio amng the native white population over 20 years of age of 20.3 percent compared with 3 percent for the Middle Atlantic States and .42 percent for New England. Reports on school attendance in 1861 point out that the number of days per person of school age in the North ranged from 49.9 to 63.5; in the South the figure was 10.6. At the outset of the Civil War the cities of Charleston, New Orleans, Memphis, and Louisville had established creditable public school systems. A few states, notably Alabama, Kentucky, Louisiana, North

Carolina, and Tennessee, had begun to make some provisions for statewide public education. However, of these only North Carolina had progressed at a rate comparable to the states of the North. It was blessed with a particularly dynamic school reformer—Calvin Wiley—as well as a state government more democratically selected and oriented and more committed to internal improvements and public education than any other in the South. Typical of the other states in the group was Alabama, whose superintendent of schools reported in 1859 that nearly half of the children were completely devoid of education.

There is another side to the story of education in the South. The very states that were virtual wastelands of common schooling were actively engaged in preparing youth from the "right" families to lead and defend the Southern way of life. By 1850 the South had more private academies than either New England or the Middle Atlantic states. Collegiate education also flourished. In the late 1850s Virginia, for example, had more colleges, more college graduates, and expended more money on higher education than Massachusetts. In most respects the curricula and climate of the Southern colleges duplicated those of their tradition-bound sister institutions of the North and West. In the South, too, there were occasional protests against the narrowness and impracticality of college studies. However, with respect to two developments in higher education, the South was unique. First, as the Civil War approached there was a growing intolerance toward the statement of ideas in any way critical of the slave system. Textbooks were expurgated and "wrongthinking" professors were threatened with dismissal.[1] Second, the decades of the 1830s, 1840s, and 1850s were

---

[1] As Professor Benjamin Hedrick of the University of North Carolina learned, one did not have to be an abolitionist to be subject to attack. In 1856 his support of the Republican presidential candidate and the free-soil cause resulted in a campaign of vilification against him by the Raleigh *Standard*, a majority of his colleagues and students, and the college's trustees.

marked by enthusiasm for military education modeled after West Point. Proponents argued that such training would provide the well-disciplined, physically fit young leadership that the section needed for the challenging years ahead.

Virginia became an early leader in military schooling when it established, under state auspices, the Virginia Military Institute in 1839. Not to be outdone, the South Carolina legislature created two such schools in 1842, the Arsenal Academy at Columbia and the Citadel Academy at Charleston. Even before these acts, a number of colleges and secondary schools throughout the South had added military studies to their offerings, and the trend continued down to the firing on Fort Sumter. In John Hope Franklin's words, "Out of these institutions, in increasing numbers, were coming the leaders who could train and command human material to serve as the bulwark of the South's defense."

The products of Southern white society and its educational system are evident in the literature of the Civil War era. There are the dashing, resourceful officers of the Confederate Army, the epitome of bravery and chivalry. Even after military defeat they would stubbornly strive to maintain as much of the old order as possible. And there are the common soldiers, the brave, ragtag, illiterate troops of wartime, the tenant farmers and sharecroppers of the future.

The tragedy of the antebellum white Southern leadership is that of a man who, with the freedom to choose, makes the wrong selections and suffers the consequences. Slavery, the failure to support education for the masses, dependence upon a one crop economy, and the decision to secede can all be declared, from the vantage point that history provides, to have been losing choices. The tragedy of the Negro is that of a man who desires for himself the fundamental elements of human dignity—freedom, respect, a job, decent housing, and opportunity for his children—who struggles to attain them but is blocked at nearly every avenue by those who despise him and are more powerful than he. One can observe this in the history of slave revolts, in reports of the conditions of freed Negroes in Northern cities and quite clearly in the history of Negro education.

During the 35-year period we are examining, the opportunities for and conditions of Negro education varied widely. It mattered greatly whether the black child was slave or free, lived in North or South or West, or resided in a rural or urban setting. But among these variables there stood one remarkably constant phenomenon: the desire for learning. So it was in 1832 when a convention of freed Negroes declared, "If we ever expect to see the influence of prejudice decrease and ourselves respected, it must be by the blessings of an enlightened education." So it was in the closing days of the Civil War when leaders of New Orleans' black community designated the education of their children as the greatest immediate need.

Mirroring the climate of Southern life and culture during the three decades prior to the Civil War, educational opportunities for Negroes below the Mason-Dixon Line became increasingly limited. Historian Carter Woodson wrote of two periods in the educational history of the antebellum Southern Negro. The first encompassed the years from the introduction of slavery to the middle 1830s, "when the majority of the people in this country answered in the affirmative the question whether or not it was prudent to educate their slaves." During that era the economic self-interest and paternalistic concerns of the masters combined with the missionary zeal of several Protestant sects to provide opportunities for literacy among the slaves. In a number of Southern cities, notably Charleston. New Orleans, Baltimore, and the District of Columbia, free Negroes established and maintained schools for their children and for poor and orphaned youth. However, by 1835, the beginning of Woodson's second period, the white leadership had reversed its position. Now they declared a little learning to be very much a dangerous thing. The activities of such educated black rebels as Denmark Vesey, David Walker and Nat Turner no doubt motivated this change of heart.[2] The prospect of slave revolts led by literate blacks, who gained inspiration from the calls for freedom of the abolitionist press, struck terror in the hearts of the planter aristocracy. Firmly committed to a cotton economy supported by the slave system, those in power were quite willing to sacrifice whatever sentimental, economic, and spiritual benefits that might accrue from the education of blacks.

Once the Southern leadership was convinced that it was "impossible to cultivate the minds of Negroes without arousing overmuch self-assertion," political influence was used to secure restrictive legislation. Throughout the South measures were enacted curbing all kinds of activities that might result in the education of Negroes and the dissemination of information among them. Masters were prohibited from teaching their slaves; schools for free Negroes were closed; in Mississippi freed Negroes were ordered to leave the state within 90 days (1831); Virginia refused to allow the return of free blacks who had gone North to obtain the education denied them at home (1838); North Carolina in 1835 prohibited the public instruction of Negroes; Georgia made it a crime to employ Negroes "in setting up type or other labor about a printing office requiring a knowledge of reading and writing." The goals and results of such policies were dramatically portrayed before the Virginia House of Delegates as early as 1832:

We have as far as possible closed every avenue by which light may enter their minds. If we could extinguish the capacity to see the light, our work would be completed; they would then be on the level with the beasts of the field and we should be safe! I am not certain that we would not do it, if we could find out the process, and that on the plea of necessity.

While the border states were less quick to legally bar the

―――――――――

[2] There is some question as to whether Turner was, in fact, literate.

schooling of Negroes, the climate against the practice was often so strong as to make teaching impossible. In the nation's capital the municipal government made no provisions for public schooling for Negroes until 1862. One can only look back with abhorrence at the extent to which the South was willing to go to protect itself behind a moat of ignorance. The cost to the Negroes is obvious, but the material, moral, and emotional price paid by white society was also considerable. The plantations of the South had for generations relied upon the utilization of literate slaves as master craftsmen, bookkeepers, and foremen. Several Southern cities had been greatly dependent on educated free Negroes, who made up a goodly percentage of the corps of mechanics, artisans, and clerks. How great was the damage done to the self-esteem and sense of moral righteousness of the South's Christian ministers, who accommodated their religious mission to the antiliteracy laws? Did they truly believe that their plan to have the Negroes memorize the essentials of faith would provide an effective alternative to reading the Bible and catechism? In the face of the accomplishments of educated Negroes, free and slave, were Southern spokesmen fully convinced of what they were attempting to convince their critics: that the blacks were incapable of learning, that they were mentally inferior?

The fact is, however, that despite the incalculable setbacks to Negro learning, these laws and hostile attitudes were not totally effective impediments. Here and there, by various means, blacks continued to learn. Secret schools were conducted in towns. In the quiet of the night hours literate house servants would transmit their knowledge to one or more slave children. There were some whites who, for selfish or noble reasons, threw caution to the wind and undertook the education of a particularly gifted Negro. Numerous black children learned their letters and numbers from very young teachers—the sons and daughters of their masters. Though often started as a lark, plantation play schools in several instances had results far more enduring than those of a mere game. Knowledge that such activity went beyond the bounds of legal propriety evidently added a note of excitement for the children. Such was the case on the plantation of John Fouchereau Grimké, judge of the Supreme Court of South Carolina, where a play school was conducted by his daughters, Sarah and Angelina. Sarah recalled the drama: "The lights were put out, the keyhole secured, and flat on our stomachs before the fire, with spelling books in our hands, we defied the laws of South Carolina."

Perhaps most remarkable are the stories of Negroes whose desire to learn was so strong and minds were so keen that they were able to teach themselves. Among them were house servants who had access to their masters' papers and books and free Negroes who worked in shops and factories, where words and figures daily passed before their eyes. One journalist visiting Savannah, Georgia reacted with mixed emotions to the number of self-educated slaves he encountered. He proclaimed it a remarkable accomplishment for the blacks, but added, "blazen it to the shame of the South, the knowledge thus acquired has been snatched from the spare records of leisure in spite of their owners' wishes and watchfulness."

In addition to a stirring record of efforts to attain literacy, the Negroes of the antebellum South offer examples of the development of ingenious alternative means of communication. The vast majority of slaves were field hands and as such denied even the limited contact with learning available to domestic servants. Yet these slaves created musical and oral literary forms of incredible beauty and richness. By means of their spirituals they conveyed not only deep religious feelings but also determination to be free. It was no coincidence that so many of these songs dealt with such Biblical themes as the exodus from Egyptian bondage, the tumbling of the walls of Jericho, and the victory of little David over Goliath. Songs, tales, and work chants, of apparently charming innocence to the ears of the white listener, often contained hidden within their lyrics satirical references to the master, messages of hope and defiance, news from distant places, plans for escape, and information regarding stops along the underground railroad. Certainly these modes of expression made a mockery of those hopes of Southern leaders that illiteracy and docility would go hand in hand.

When the war came, Negroes and whites in the North organized freedmen's aid societies to provide food, clothing, medical assistance, and schooling for the newly emancipated slaves. They found the Southern blacks not merely receptive to the idea of education but, as in the previously mentioned case of New Orleans, wildly enthusiastic for it. In September, 1861 the first of the society sponsored institutions was opened at Fortress Monroe, Virginia by Mrs. Mary Peake, daughter of a Negro mother and white father. The school was run under the auspices of the American Missionary Association with the active cooperation of the military government. This kind of joint effort became familiar throughout the South. There were also examples of the military taking the initiative in launching an educational program. The public school system for freedmen in New Orleans and vicinity is a case in point. In a number of locales schools were set up by teachers acting independent of outside support or authority. Mary Chase, a free Negro of Alexandria, Virginia, founded a school in that town two weeks prior to the opening of Mrs. Peake's at Fortress Monroe. Finally, those courageous white and Negro teachers, who for years had been conducting schools in secret, now brought their institutions into the open and continued to serve the blacks on a larger scale than ever.

The future of education for the Negroes in the South looked extremely promising in the early months of 1865. With the establishment of the Freedmens Bureau the federal government assumed major responsibility for encouraging, coordinating, and supervising the schooling of the former slaves. Under the Bureau's auspices hundreds of thousands of dollars would be expended for the cause, teachers would be brought south from the common schools of New England, and, for Negro and white children alike, the tide of illiteracy would begin to turn.

That the end of Reconstruction brought severe setbacks is well known. The details of that story do not fall within the sphere of this volume. However, let it be noted that the desire for and determination to attain knowledge, which the Negro of the South had demonstrated throughout the decades of slavery, remained ever constant in the years that followed.

To this day the forms of prejudice against blacks in the North differ in certain respects from those in the South. Nevertheless, wherever he travels in this country, the Negro finds himself the victim of racism. For many Northern whites it took the urban upheavals of the 1960s for this to finally penetrate, but the condition has, in fact, existed since colonial times. It is true that in the North during the pre-Civil War decades there were found men passionately dedicated to the abolishment of slavery. Yet, up to the very eve of the conflict they were widely considered to be troublemakers and rabblerousers, whose cause was injurious to public safety and the preservation of the Union. In the middle 1830s respectable Northerners joined with their Southern brethren to express shock at what they considered abolitionist attempts to inflame slaves to revolt. For example, on August 21, 1835 some of Boston's most prominent citizens met at Faneuil Hall to denounce the Anti-Slavery Society. Men like Peley Sprague, Richard Fletcher, Theodore Lyman, Jr., Harrison Gray Otis, and Edward Everett demanded laws to curb the activities of the abolitionist "fanatics."

One might presume that for many Northerners criticizing abolitionists provided a convenient, socially acceptable cover for blocking Negro aspirations. News of slave plots and revolts undoubtedly reinforced long held fears of Negro violence in Northern urban centers. The Southern argument that Negroes were intellectually and morally inferior was received with many an affirmative nod north of Dixie. Such a view could be found in literature and in school texts authored by New Englanders. There is every reason to suspect that at the roots of Northern attitudes toward blacks and their supporters was what Samuel

Ringgold Ward called "the ever present, ever crushing, Negro-hate."[3]

Restrictions upon educational opportunities for Negroes in the North tended to be most direct and most virulent in those cases in which abolitionist sponsors were involved and in areas of sparse Negro population, where whites feared their inmigration. Such was the case in little Canaan, New Hampshire during the spring of 1835. There Noyes Academy, whose board of trustees included several abolitionists, opened its doors for the first time. Among the 42 students in attendance were 14 Negroes whose tuitions had been paid by the Anti-Slavery Society. It was the desire of the sponsors "to afford colored youths fair opportunity to show that they are capable, equally with the whites, of improving themselves in every social virtue, and every Christian ornament."

Unfortunately, the school was denied the opportunity to achieve this noble goal. The citizens of Canaan were incensed at the presence of a body of blacks in their midst and feared a mass influx in the future. By official action of the town meeting on August 10, 1835 the academy's building was physically removed from its foundation and dragged by a hundred yoke of oxen onto the town common. This was done in "the interest of the town, the *honor* of the State, and the *good* of the whole community." The action followed months of rumors that the school would attract hordes of fugitive slaves to the town. As one commentator wrote, "Fourteen black boys with books in their hands set the entire Granite state crazy."

Another dramatic example of intolerance took place, beginning in 1832, in Canterbury, Connecticut, when Prudence Crandall accepted a young Negro girl into her otherwise all-white boarding school. Parents of the student body immediately protested, and, after Miss Crandall refused to act on their demand

---

[3] Ward, a Negro minister, grew up in New York City during the Jacksonian era.

that the "nigger" be removed, most of them withdrew their daughters. Their action only strengthened Miss Crandall's resolve. With the advice and support of William Lloyd Garrison and other leading abolitionists, she decided to convert her school into one exclusively "for young colored Ladies and Misses."

The reaction of the townspeople was overwhelmingly hostile. Even before the reconstituted school opened its doors, efforts were made, in accordance with the decision of a town meeting, to dissuade Miss Crandall. She was informed that her school would bring about "injurious effects, and incalculable evils." She was not, however, completely lacking supporters. The Rev. Samuel J. May had spoken out on her behalf at the town meeting, insisting that education was a fundamental right of all men and warning the townspeople that in denying Negroes their rights they were endangering their own. Nevertheless, the position of selectman Andrew J. Judson proved far more convincing and had won the day. An active member of the colonization society, Judson urged that Negroes belonged not in Connecticut but in Africa, where they could be of immeasurable aid to their fellows by bringing them the fruits of Christian civilization. In America, he argued, they were by reason of their inherent inferiority destined to occupy servile positions.

Miss Crandall refused to budge, and the abolitionists rallied to support a *cause célèbre*. In April, 1833 the school reopened with a complement of Negro young ladies drawn from the major Eastern cities. Almost immediately a campaign of harassment was launched by the townspeople. Students were insulted on the streets; medical aid was denied; local merchants refused to supply the school's needs; the school's well was contaminated with cow dung. When these and other acts failed to break the spirit of Miss Crandall and her girls, the town government considered imposing the vagrancy law. This gave the town selectmen power to order any out-of-state resident to deposit or pay a fine of $1.67 for each week he remained after receiving notice to depart from the town. Finally, however, the decision was made to appeal to the state legislature for aid in removing the "nigger school."

On May 24th the legislature accommodated the good people of Canterbury with a law prohibiting the establishment of a school for "colored persons who are not inhabitants of this state" and the instructing, harboring, or boarding of such persons without the written consent of local authorities. Under this law's authority Miss Crandall was subsequently arrested. The first trial, held on August 23rd, resulted in a hung jury. The second, two months later, ended with a verdict of guilty. However, the final decision was handed down by an appellate court on July 22, 1834. On the technical grounds of defects in the information submitted by the state's attorney, the conviction was overturned.

For Miss Crandall and her supporters the victory was far from complete. The appellate court failed to rule on the constitutionality of the "Black Law" of 1833, and the townspeople refused to lift their siege against the school. In the face of continuing attempts to destroy the school building, Miss Crandall finally capitulated. On September 10, 1834 she closed her school and left Canterbury and Connecticut forever. Yet there is an epilogue to this story that offers evidence that man can in the name of justice rise above his prejudices. The chairman of the legislative committee responsible for proposing the 1833 law in time acknowledged that the act was contrary "to the dictates of common humanity and justice." He initiated a petition that successfully led to the statute's repeal in May of 1838.

There were other instances of direct action by local whites to prevent the establishment of Negro schools during the 1830s. For example, an attempt to institute a manual labor college for blacks in New Haven was abandoned after a town meeting declared that "the founding of colleges for educating colored people is an unwarrantable and dangerous undertaking to the internal concerns of other states and ought to be discouraged, and that the mayor, alderman, common council, and freemen will resist the movement by every lawful means." In the Ohio towns of Zanesville and Troy, Negro schools were destroyed by local mobs. Nevertheless, despite such setbacks, schools continued to be organized throughout the North, and in most cases they were able to withstand the hostility of white residents.

With the onset of the common-school crusade, Negroes and their abolitionist allies concentrated a good deal of their efforts on obtaining an adequate portion of public funds for the schooling of black children. While public schools had been synonymous with charity, pauper education, Negroes had generally kept away from them. As Woodson pointed out, they wished to avoid the stigma of being branded as public charges. The evolution of the concept of free public schools for all children understandably altered their position. Not only was there a desire to have their youth share the great opportunities which reformers promised would be among the fruits of the common school, but there was also the matter of their right as taxpayers to benefit from an institution their taxes helped support.

The opportunities for black children to attend public schools in the North was by no means universal throughout this period. Not until the 1850s did the legislatures of Ohio, Illinois, Iowa, Michigan, and Wisconsin require that school funds be made available for Negroes. The arguments against such appropriations usually included the old standby that the Negro was intellectually inferior, and thus expenditures for their education would be a waste. There was also the very effective contention that free schools would likely encourage further Negro migration, a consequence that would be highly unpopular among voters and that, it was stressed, would impede African colonization, antagonize the South, and further endanger the Union. While they struggled to overcome restrictive educational laws, Negroes and white abolitionists continued to establish and support schools at their own expense. In Ohio and Illinois particularly, the enthusiasm with which they engaged in these endeavors and the progress of the children did much to weaken the opposition arguments based upon racist stereotypes of unambitious, ineffectual, mentally inferior Negroes.

While the cause of justice eventually succeeded in procuring publicly supported schooling for the blacks of the free states, the grip of racism on the minds of most citizens was by no means broken. With few exceptions Negro children were denied by law or custom seats in the "common" school of children from all classes, all religions, and all ethnic groups. The public schools they attended were segregated and usually inadequately and inequitably financed. Negro teachers generally were paid salaries even lower than those of their white colleagues. Terms like "caste schools" and "painfully neglected" were used by contemporary observers to describe the "colored" schools. In New York City the 1857 report of the Society for the Promotion of Education Among Colored Children found white children attending school in "splendid, almost palatial edifices," while Negro youth were "pent up in filthy neighborhoods, in old and dilapidated buildings." Conditions such as these were the consequence of a budget that, despite a ratio of 1 Negro child for every 40 whites in the schools, allocated funds on the basis of 1 to 1600.

School segregation was the product of racism. Most often it was imposed on the Negro community by the white majority. Yet there were instances in the 1830s of Negroes in some Eastern cities petitioning for separate educational facilities. The memorial to the New York State legislature of a group of Rochester Negroes and white sympathizers in 1832 informs us of the motives for such requests:

Under the present organization our schools are open to all, and yet it is obvious that in them the literary and moral interest of the colored scholar can hardly prosper. He is reproached with his color; he is taunted with his origin, and if permitted to mingle with others in the joyous pastimes of youth, it is of favor, not of right. Thus the law which may declare him free, now or in prospect, may be a dead letter. His energies are confined, his hopes are crushed, his mind is in chains, and he is still a slave.

The legislature responded by granting permission for the establishment in Rochester of one or more Negro schools and allocating state funds for their partial support.

During the three decades prior to the Civil War the Negro communities of the Northeast often divided over the issue of separate schools. As in the case of Rochester, some saw Negro public schools as providing the only possible environment in which their children could peaceably pursue their studies. Others would have opted for integration if the opportunity was available but, rather than fight the system, chose to devote their full efforts to securing additional funds and improved facilities for the black schools. Increasingly, the more militant and dynamic Negro leaders together with white abolitionists placed themselves in strong opposition to segregation.[4] Separatism, they insisted, was not only demeaning to the race but conducive to inferior education since whites would never willingly provide adequate funds for Negro schools.

The most significant, direct, and dramatic struggle against segregated public schooling took place in Boston. The fact that this city, the very capital of the antislavery movement, was by the middle 1840s the only Massachusetts community that still required its Negro children to attend separate "colored schools" was particularly irritating to abolitionist leaders. In 1844 a group of prominent Boston abolitionists appealed to the Primary School Committee for the admission of Negro children to regular classes. A majority on the Committee responded negatively on the grounds that natural distinctions existed among races, established by "the All-Wise Creator," that "no

---

[4] Beginning in 1847 Frederick Douglass played a major role in a campaign to convince Rochester's Negroes and school officials to reverse their position on segregated schooling. In 1856 the city's "colored school" was finally abandoned.

legislature, no social customs, can efface" and that "renders a promiscuous intermingling in the public schools disadvantageous both to them and to the whites." They also called attention to the dangers of integration in light of "the present state of public feelings and sentiment." The minority report, on the other hand, stressed the needless costs of supporting a dual school system and the moral damage to the white children who daily witnessed the example of official prejudice based on color alone. Furthermore, they argued that forced segregation was illegal, since schools were the common property of all, designed for the use of all. While legal precedents allowed distinctions to be made on the grounds of age and sex, separation on the basis of color, they insisted, was contrary both to the letter of the law and the spirit of the common-school ideal.

Despite this setback before the Primary School Committee, attacks against segregation in Boston continued, particularly in the pages of the abolitionist newspaper *The Liberator*. The next act in the drama was played in the courts. In 1848 Benjamin Roberts, a Negro, sued the city on behalf of his five-year-old daughter Sarah. Having unsuccessfully sought four times to enroll her in a white primary school, he was obliged to send the child to a distant Negro school. Roberts' lawyers, Charles Sumner, the future United States senator, and Negro attorney Robert Morris, based their case upon a statute that permitted any person illegally excluded from the public schools to receive damage payment from the city. In his forceful presentation to the state's supreme court Sumner insisted that segregated schools violated the equal rights provisions of the state constitution, that the education obtained in such schools was inherently unequal, since "a school, exclusively devoted to one class, must differ essentially, in its spirit and character, from that public school ... where all classes meet together in equality." He also reasserted the argument that segregated education was damaging to white children as well as to blacks.

Once again the right to establish and maintain segregated schools was upheld. In its unanimous decision delivered by

Chief Justice Lemuel Shaw, the court held that the Primary School Committee's legal responsibility was to provide for the "colored" population schools "as well fitted, in point of capacity and qualification of instructors, to advance the education of children under seven years old, as the other primary schools. . . ." Since, in the court's opinion, this had in fact been done for Negro children, including Sarah Roberts, no legal damages had occurred. Before concluding, Justice Shaw directed his remarks to one of Sumner's most compelling arguments:

It is urged, that this maintenance of separate schools tends to deepen and perpetuate the odious distinction of caste, founded in a deep-rooted prejudice in public opinion. This prejudice, if it exists, is not created by law, and probably cannot be changed by law. Whether this distinction and prejudice, existing in the opinion and feeling of the community, would not be also effectually fostered by compelling colored and white children to associate together in the same schools, may well be doubted; at all events, it is a fair and proper question for the Committee to consider and decide upon, having in view the best interests of both classes of children under their superintendence, and we cannot say, that their decision upon it is not founded on just grounds of reason and experience, and in the results of a discriminating and honest judgement.

As Leon Litwack notes in writing of the Roberts case, "The importance of the decision transcended the local struggle. . . . Shaw's legal defense of segregated schools on the basis of the 'separate but equal' doctrine established a controversial precedent in American law." Not until *Brown* v. *Board of Education* in 1954 was it finally reversed. For the Negroes of Boston, however, the wait was far shorter. Organizing the Equal School Rights Committee, they exerted continuous pressure on the city and state governments to legislate separate schools out of existence. On April 28, 1855 the governor of Massachusetts signed an act prohibiting racial and religious bars to admission to public schools.

The entry of Negro students into previously all-white schools the following September marked the successful conclusion of a 15-year campaign. For the nation as a whole the struggle had two consequences that were vastly different from each other. As noted above, the "separate but equal" doctrine, which helped establish legal support for decades of segregated schooling, particularly in the South, originated in the Roberts case. On the other hand, in the months and years immediately following the victory of the integration forces, the Boston example lent encouragement to Negroes in other Northern cities and towns. In a number of communities with relatively small Negro populations, agitation did result in integrated schooling. However, at the time of the issuance of the Emancipation Proclamation, Boston alone among the nation's major cities had eliminated separate Negro schools. Arguments stressing the injustice and immorality of segregated schooling could, at times, stimulate local authorities to the point of expending more money to improve their "colored" schools, but integration was another matter. There is little evidence that this was an attractive prospect to the white majority even at the moment that its sons were engaged in battle against the confederacy of slave states. In the middle of the nineteenth century many considered it not at all inconsistent to oppose slavery as immoral while simultaneously voicing belief in the inferiority of the Negro people and fear of racial amalgamation. This had been the position of Thomas Jefferson right up to the time of his death in 1826. It was also possibly the view of the New York *Herald*, which responded to school integration in Boston with the cry:

Now the blood of the Winthrops, the Otises, the Lymans, the Endicotts, and the Eliots, is in fair way to be amalgamated with the Sambos, the Catos, and the Pompeys. The North is to be Africanized. Amalgamation has commenced. New England heads the column. God save the Commonwealth of Massachu-setts!

The struggle by Northern blacks to attain equal educational opportunities for their children attests both to the courage and persistence of these persecuted people and to the powerful attraction of the common-school ideal. It further tends to substantiate the fact that public schools generally reflect the values and aspirations of the majority. No matter how sincere reformers might have been in their desire to make the common school common to all, society determined that the Negro was to be considered an exception. Here he was denied access to schooling; there he was placed in segregated and inferior institutions, and even in the few localities where he attended school with white children, he often was required to sit among his fellow blacks, apart from the rest of the class.

The experiences of the Negro also presented some serious challenges to his own hopes and to reformers' assurances that in providing free public schooling society was offering a significant opportunity for all to climb the ladder of success. As has been noted, segregated schooling was inferior schooling, thus immediately eliminating the Negro child from obtaining the full benefits of public education. Negro parents often were unable to provide proper clothing with which to send their children to school. Others were forced, out of sheer economic necessity, to withdraw their sons and daughters from school and put them to work. One New Yorker noted in 1859, "It is a common complaint of colored teachers that their pupils are taken from school at the very time their studies become most useful and attractive." In the pre-Civil War era approximately half of the Negroes in Philadelphia and New York had received no formal schooling at all. Finally, as historian Gilbert Osofsky convincingly put it, education, "segregated or integrated," was of limited value "to a youngster whose economic vistas were limited to jobs for beggarly paid menials." In 1830 a teacher of Negro children spoke of this tragic situation in vivid terms:

*After a boy has spent five or six years in the school and ... is
spoken of in terms of high approbation by respectable visitors
... he leaves school, with every avenue closed against him,
which is open to the white boy for honorable and respectable
rank in society, doomed to encounter as much prejudice and
contempt, as if he were not only destitute of that education
... but as if he were incapable of receiving it.*

It cannot be denied that there were some gains made during
this era. In addition to those already discussed, one can point
to areas of progress in higher education. Three Negro colleges
were founded: Avery College in Pennsylvania in 1849, Ashman
Institute (later changed to Lincoln University) in Pennsylvania
in 1854, and the next year Wilberforce University in Ohio. By
1860 a number of previously all-white colleges, medical schools,
and theological seminaries in the North had opened their gates
to Negro students. But as the Negro children attending integrated public schools in a handful of towns were exceptions to
the rule, even more so were the black youth who could overcome poverty, obtain a decent college preparatory education,
and aspire to higher education, when all evidence pointed to
the likelihood that they would be denied the full benefits of
their scholarly labors. Throughout the antebellum period
Negro spokesmen made it quite clear that among the things
they desired most for their race was equal opportunity for
quality schooling followed by equal opportunity to enter the
trades and professions. To this day they have been denied
these goals; to this day they have persisted in their efforts to
realize them.

conclusion

It was appropriate that the federal government in 1865 chose to include education among the resources brought South to help reconstruct that devastated region. For more than 35 years reformers had impressed upon the American mind a belief in the redeeming powers of schooling. Over this period they had effected dramatic changes in the educational scene.

Prior to the 1830s inequities prevailed in the opportunity to obtain elementary schooling, dependent upon such factors as place of residence, income, class, and race. At the outset of an era marked by the extension of political democracy, publicly sponsored schools generally bore the stigma of institutions for the indigent. While the last ties between church and state were being severed, many continued to advocate a primary role for religion in the sponsorship and control of schooling. In rural frontier areas as well as in the emerging industrial centers there were those who argued that children whose life work was to be at a machine or behind a plow had little need for even the rudiments of learning. Yet, despite these and other obstacles, by 1865 all the states outside the South had achieved or were on the threshold of establishing universal, tax-supported, free common schooling.

The common-school crusade was a remarkable phenomenon, of lasting significance. Beginning in the era of the Manns and Barnards the concept of education as a right available to all citizens emerged. It has since grown to the point where the United States has provided more schooling for more people than any other nation in history. Public schools must be given major credit for the spread of literacy throughout the population, a gift whose value to individuals and society is immeasurable. It is in vogue these days to stress the differences that divide our populace along racial, ethnic, and class lines; however, one cannot ignore, even if he chooses to deprecate, the value system and general outlook that mark Americans as a people. Long before the advent of radio, television, and other media of mass communication, these were being shaped to a large degree in the schoolrooms across the land. So many of the educational practices we today categorize as progressive were initially advocated by the educational pioneers of the middle nineteenth century: more humane and realistic approaches to childhood, more effective tools and techniques of teaching, more meaningful and utilitarian studies at all levels of schooling, and extension of educational opportunities for women, to name a few. It is no wonder that students today who read the works of those men and women express amazement at how modern their ideas appear.

Ultimately of no less significance than their theories concerning the nature and optimum conditions of education were the reformers' expressions of confidence in the power of schooling to cure social and moral ills and create a just and prosperous society. The course of time has led to the extension of the number of years of education deemed necessary to prepare youth to achieve these noble ends, but the faith has persisted. Since the inception of the common schools, learning for learning's sake, for the development of loyalty to church and/or state, as preparation for life work—what might be termed traditional objectives—have failed to elicit the kind of enthusiastic support that attends demands that our educational system bear the major burden of substantially alleviating such concerns as crime, poverty, alcoholism, racism, or a technological gap between our nation and a foreign competitor. This has not only presented education with often impossible tasks to perform, but it has also obstructed effective reform by distracting attention from the root causes of problems.

From time immemorial schools have functioned as agencies for propagating and preserving dominant cultural values. As such they invariably are conservative institutions, resistant to change, indeed as we have seen, often lagging behind a rapidly moving society. A common educational experience, despite the hopes of reformers, did not guarantee equal opportunity for all to achieve success in life. The school's effectiveness as a ladder up has generally been dependent upon the welcome awaiting the individual at the top. As society's agent, the school could not negate society's barriers to those whose class, religious, sex, or racial credentials were not acceptable. Even the public school itself could not escape the impact of those biases. They have been reflected in inequities in the quality of public education. They have been expressed in the certainty of superiority with which middle-class, Protestant, Anglo-Saxon values have been imposed upon those whose heritage differed from that of the majority.

It is, therefore, not for furthering an image of schooling as a panacea for society's problems that we look back on the leaders of the educational reform movement with respect and admiration. Instead it is for making learning accessible to more people of all ages and stations of life and for identifying for their own and future generations ways in which education could evolve more and more into a rewarding venture. For those who held comfortable positions in American society, schooling became a more effective instrument for status maintenance. For many struggling to overcome social and economic deprivation, education emerged more than ever as a significant part of the good life they sought.

bibliographic note

Chapter One: A Climate for Reform

Among the works from which I have drawn my description of the general climate of Jacksonian America are Edward Pessen, *Jacksonian America: Society, Personality, and Politics* (Homewood, Ill.: Dorsey, 1969), Arthur M. Schlesinger, Jr., *The Age of Jackson* (Boston: Little, Brown, 1945), and Glyndon G. Van Deusen, *The Jacksonian Era, 1828–1948* (New York: Harper and Row, 1959). Two social histories that have been particularly useful are Merle Curti, *The Growth of American Thought* (New York: Harper and Bros., 1943) and Nelson M. Blake, *A History of American Life and Thought* (New York: McGraw-Hill, 1963). An invaluable study of American culture and social habits during the antebellum period is Douglas Branch, *The Sentimental Years, 1830–1860* (New York: Appleton-Century, 1934).

For my discussion of urban growth I have used Charles M. Glaab and A. Theodore Brown, *A History of Urban America* (New York: Macmillan, 1967) and Constance McLaughlin Green, *The Rise of Urban America* (New York: Harper and Row, 1967). An outstanding study of the growth of trans-

Appalachian cities is Richard C. Wade, *The Urban Frontier: The Rise of Western Cities, 1790–1830* (Cambridge: Harvard University Press, 1959).

The best general account of the humanitarian reform movement of the era is Alice F. Tyler, *Freedom's Ferment: Phases of American Social History to 1860* (Minneapolis: University of Minnesota Press, 1944). Much of my discussion of this phenomenon is also drawn from Curti, *American Thought* (op. cit.), Blake, *American Life* (op. cit.) and Branch, *Sentimental Years* (op. cit.).

A landmark in the writing of American educational history, and a most valuable source of information for the background and development of the common-school movement, is Lawrence A. Cremin, *The American Common School, An Historical Conception* (New York: Teachers College Press, 1951). A work that is extremely useful for its treatment of the political manifestations of school reform is Rush Welter, *Popular Education and Democratic Thought in America* (New York: Columbia University Press, 1962). An excellent discussion of the motives and aims of school reform is contained in Robert H. Wiebe, "The Social Functions of Public Education," *American Quarterly*, Vol. XXI, No. 2, Pt. 1 (Summer 1969).

In addition to the above works, information regarding the condition of education in the several states is based largely upon Frank Tracy Carlton, *Economic Influences upon Educational Progress in the United States, 1820–1860* (Madison: University of Wisconsin Press, 1908; reissued by Teachers College Press, 1965). A useful source on education in the South and cited in the chapter is Clement Eaton, *The Freedom-of-Thought Struggle in the Old South* (New York: Harper and Row, 1964). The discussion of schooling in Illinois is based upon John Pulliam's informative article "Changing Attitudes Toward Free Public Schools in Illinois, 1825–1860," *History of Education Quarterly*, Vol. VII, No. 2 (Summer 1967).

Chapter Two: A Crusade Emerges

My discussion of Pestalozzi's philosophy and educational ventures is drawn from excerpts of his writings found in Frederick M. Binder (ed.), *Education in the History of Western Civilization: Selected Readings* (New York: Macmillan, 1970). A thorough study of the Swiss reformer is Gerald L. Gutek, *Pestalozzi and Education* (New York: Random House, 1968). Most helpful for its treatment of early Pestalozzian influences in America is H. G. Good, *A History of American Education* (New York: Macmillan, 1956).

Passages from the writings of Horace Mann are from selections found in Lawrence Cremin (ed.), *The Republic and the School: Horace Mann on the Education of Free Men* (New York: Teachers College Press, 1957), Binder, *Education in the History of Western Civilization* (op. cit.), and *Life and Works of Horace Mann* (Boston: Lee and Shepard, 1891).

The most useful source for my discussion of the workingmen's movement has been Edward Pessen, *Most Uncommon Jacksonians: The Radical Leaders of the Early Labor Movement* (Albany: State University of New York Press, 1967). Other contributors are R. V. Curoe, *Educational Attitudes and Policies of Organized Labor in the United States* (New York: Teachers College, 1926) and Sidney Jackson, "Labor, Education and Politics in the 1830's," *Pennsylvania Magazine of History and Biography*, Vol. LXVI, No. 3 (July 1942). For a revisionist interpretation of labor's contribution to the common-school cause see Jay M. Pawa, "The Attitude of Labor Organizations in New York State Toward Public Education, 1829–1890 (Unpublished Ed. D. project, Teachers College, Columbia, 1964) and Jay M. Pawa, "Workingmen and Free Schools in the Nineteenth Century: A Comment on the Labor-Education Thesis," *History of Education Quarterly*, Vol. XI, No. 3 (Fall 1971).

Most of what I have written on the role of major political parties in the education movement is based upon Welter, *Popular Education* (op. cit.). In discussing the motives of middle-class Whig reformers I used Charles E. Bidwell, "The Moral Significance of the Common School," *History of Education Quarterly*, Vol. III, No. 3 (Fall 1966).

For my biographical sketch of Horace Mann and discussion of his philosophy I have found most useful Merle Curti, *The Social Ideas of American Educators* (New York: Scribner, 1935), Lawrence Cremin, "Horace Mann's Legacy" in *The Republic and the School* (op. cit.), and Jonathan Messerli, *Horace Mann: A Biography* (New York: Alfred A. Knopf, 1972). Also consulted were Mary Peabody Mann, *Life of Horace Mann* (Boston: Walker, Fuller, 1865), Louise Hall Tharp, *Until Victory: Horace Mann and Mary Peabody* (Boston: Little, Brown, 1953), and E.I.F. Williams, *Horace Mann: Educational Statesmen* (New York: Macmillan, 1937).

The most complete study of phrenology is John D. Davies, *Phrenology: Fad and Science: A 19th-Century American Crusade* (New Haven: Yale University Press, 1955). I also found the discussion in Branch, *Sentimental Years* (op. cit.) helpful.

Chapter Three: Issues of Controversy, Fruits of Victory

My accounts of Mann's conflicts with his several critics are based upon Cremin, *American Common School* (op. cit.), Raymond B. Culver, *Horace Mann and Religion in the Massachusetts Public Schools* (New Haven: Yale University Press, 1929), Neil G. McCluskey, *Public Schools and Moral Education* (New York: Columbia University Press, 1951), and Welter, *Popular Education* (op. cit.).

The most comprehensive study of anti-Catholic sentiment is Ray Allen Billington, *The Protestant Crusade, 1800–1860* (New York: Macmillan, 1938). For my discussion of the religious controversies in New York and Philadelphia I used Vincent P. Lannie, *Public Money and Parochial Education: Bishop Hughes, Governor Seward, and the New York School Controversy* (Cleveland: Press of Case Western University, 1968), Vincent P. Lannie, "William Seward and the New York School Controversy, 1840–1842: A Problem in Historical Motivation," *History of Education Quarterly*, Vol. VI, No. 1 (Spring 1966), John W. Pratt, "Governor Seward and the New York School Controversy, 1840–1842," *New York History*, Vol. XLII, No. 1 (October 1961), and Vincent P. Lannie and Bernard C. Diethorn, "For the Honor and Glory of God: The Philadelphia Bible Riots of 1840," *History of Education Quarterly*, Vol. VIII, No. 1 (Spring 1968).

An excellent discussion of the role of religion in school reform in the West is found in David Tyack, "The Kingdom of God and the Common Schools," *Harvard Education Review*, Vol. XXXVI, No. 4 (Fall 1966). Pulliam, "Changing Attitudes" (op. cit.) also considers this subject. A fascinating case study of intolerance is William B. Faherty, S.J., "Nativism and Midwestern Education: The Experience of Saint Louis University, 1832–1856," *History of Education Quarterly*, Vol. VII, No. 4 (Winter 1968).

For my discussion of changing attitudes toward childhood and child nurture I used Bernard Wishy, *The Child and the Republic: The Dawn of Modern American Child Nurture* (Philadelphia: University of Pennsylvania Press, 1968) and Branch, *Sentimental Years* (op. cit.).

Interesting studies of the status of woman in the American mind are Barbara Welter, "The Cult of True Womanhood, 1820–1860," *American Quarterly*, Vol. XVIII, No. 2, Pt. 1 (Summer 1966) and Glenda Riley, "Origins of the Argument for Improved Female Education," *History of Education Quarterly*, Vol. IX, No. 4 (Winter 1969).

My account of the feminizing of the teaching profession and the establishment of normal schools is based upon Merle L. Borrowman (ed.), *Teacher Education in America: A Documentary History* (New York: Teachers College Press, 1965), Merle L. Borrowman, *The Liberal and Technical in Teacher Education: A Historical Survey of American Thought* (New York: Teachers College Press, 1956), Branch, *Sentimental Years* (op. cit.), J. P. Gordy, *Rise and Growth of the Normal School Idea in the United States* (Washington, D.C.: Govt. Printing

Office, Bureau of Education, 1891), Michael B. Katz, *The Irony of Early School Reform: Educational Innovation in Mid-Nineteenth Century Massachusetts* (Cambridge: Harvard University Press, 1968), Wiebe, "The Social Functions of Public Education" (op. cit.), and Charles A. Harper, *A Century of Public Teacher Education* (Washington, D.C.: National Education Association, 1939).

For my discussion of teachers' associations, journals, and institutes I used Sidney L. Jackson, *America's Struggle for Free Schools: Social Tension and Education in New England and New York, 1827–1842* (Washington, D.C.: American Council on Public Affairs, 1941) and Kenneth V. Lottich, "Educational Leadership in Early Ohio," *History of Education Quarterly,* Vol. II, No. 1 (March 1962).

My summary of educational progress in the several states is largely based upon the same sources cited for the earlier survey in Chapter One, with the addition of Lottich, "Educational Leadership" (op. cit.) and Good, *A History of American Education* (op. cit.). For information on Henry Barnard's activities in Connecticut and Rhode Island I consulted Curti, *Social Ideas of American Educators* (op. cit.) and Bernard C. Steiner, *Life of Henry Barnard* (Washington, D.C.: Bureau of Education, Bul. 1919, No. 8, Government Printing Office, 1919).

An excellent analysis of the content and values expressed in nineteenth century textbooks is provided in Ruth Miller Elson, *Guardians of Tradition: American Schoolbooks of the Nineteenth Century* (Lincoln, Nebraska: University of Nebraska Press, 1964). A thorough study of the most popular American reader is Richard D. Mosier, *Making of the American Mind: Social and Moral Ideas in the McGuffey Readers* (New York: Kings Crown, 1947). I also found useful information on schoolbooks and juvenile literature in Clifton Johnson, *Old-Time Schools and School-Books* (New York: Macmillan, 1904), Wishy, *Child and the Republic* (op. cit.), and Branch, *Sentimental Years* (op. cit.).

Chapter Four: Beyond the Common School

My account of the academy is based to a considerable extent upon Theodore Sizer (ed.), *The Age of the Academies* (New York: Teachers College Press, 1964). Also helpful were Elmer Ellsworth Brown, *The Making of Our Middle Schools* (New York: Longmans, Green, 1914) and James McLachlan, *American Boarding Schools: A Historical Study* (New York: Scribner, 1970).

Michael Katz's study of school reform in Massachusetts, *Irony of Early School Reform* (op. cit.), has been an invaluable source for my discussion and interpretation of the high-school movement. In addition I used Brown, *The Making of Our Middle Schools* (op. cit.), Emit D. Grizzell, *Origin and Development of the High School in New England Before 1865* (New York: Macmillan, 1923), and Robert G. Hahn and David B. Bidna (eds.), *Secondary Education: Origin and Directions* (New York: Macmillan, 1965).

James McLachlan's acclaimed work on the history of the boarding school, *American Boarding Schools* (op. cit.), was the most important source for my discussion of that institution.

For my treatment of the kindergarten I used Nina C. Vandewalker, *The Kindergarten in American Education* (New York: Macmillan, 1908). Excerpts of Froebel's writings are from Binder, *Education in the History of Western Civilization* (op. cit.).

Books dealing with the work of Edward Sheldon at Oswego are Ned H. Dearborn, *The Oswego Movement in American Education* (New York: Teachers College Press, 1951) and Andrew P. Hollis, *The Contributions of the Oswego Normal School to Educational Progress in the United States* (Boston: Heath, 1898).

Among the several sources consulted for my treatment of higher education Frederick Rudolph's, *The American College and University, A History* (New York: Random House, 1962) proved most valuable. Donald G. Tewksbury's *The Founding of American Universities and Colleges Before the Civil War* (New York: Teachers College, 1937) provides a wealth of vital statistics. My discussion of Francis Wayland is based largely on Richard Hofstadter and Hardy C. DeWitt, *The Development and Scope of Higher Education in the United States* (New York: Columbia University Press, 1952). A comprehensive account of the history of the Morrill Act is found in Edward D. Eddy, Jr., *Colleges for Our Land and Time: The Land-Grant Idea in American Education* (New York: Harper and Row, 1957). I also found most useful John H. Florer, "Major Issues in the Congressional Debate of the Morrill Act of 1862," *History of Education Quarterly*, Vol. VIII, No. 4 (Winter 1968). For my discussion of higher education for women I used Merle Curti, *Social Ideas of American Education* (op. cit.), Thomas Woody, *A History of Women's Education in the United States* (New York: Science Press, 1929), and Barbara M. Cross (ed.), *The Educated Woman in America* (New York: Teachers College Press, 1965). An excellent source of documents in the history of higher education is Richard Hofstadter and Wilson Smith (eds.), *American Higher Education: A Documentary History* (Chicago: University of Chicago Press, 1961).

The most comprehensive study of the lyceum movement is Carl Bode, *The American Lyceum: Town Meeting of the Mind* (New York: Oxford University Press, 1956). A brief, earlier history is Cecil B. Hayes, *The American Lyceum: Its History and Contribution to Education* (Washington, D.C.: U.S. Office of Education, Bul. No. 12, Government Printing Office, 1932). Excerpts from Holbrook's writings are contained in C. Hartley Gratton (ed.), *American Ideas About Adult Education, 1710– 1951* (New York: Teachers College Press, 1956). Also useful is Malcom S. Knowles, *The Adult Education Movement in the United States* (New York: Holt, Rinehart and Winston, 1962).

For the history of the library movement I used Sidney Ditzion, *Arsenals of a Democratic Culture* (Chicago: American Library Association, 1947) and Jesse H. Shera, *Foundations of the Public Library: The Origins of the Public Library Movement in New England, 1629–1855* (Chicago: University of Chicago Press, 1949).

Chapter Five: Other Places, Other People

Rush Welter, *Popular Education* (op. cit.) provides an excellent analysis of the Southern political climate as it related to school reform. John Hope Franklin's *The Militant South, 1800–1861* (Cambridge: Belknap, 1956) offers a detailed description and analysis of the rise of military schools in the South. Other works used for my treatment of Southern education are Eaton, *Freedom-of-Thought Struggle* (op. cit.), William R. Taylor, "Toward a Definition of Orthodoxy: The Patrician South and the Common Schools," *Harvard Education Review*, Vol. XXXVI, No. 4 (Fall 1966), Irving Gershenberg, "Southern Values and Public Education: A Revision," *History of Education Quarterly*, Vol. X, No. 4 (Winter 1970), and Curti, *Social Ideas of American Educators* (op. cit.).

The most comprehensive study of antebellum Negro education is Carter Woodson's classic *The Education of the Negro Prior to 1861* (Washington, D.C.: Associated Publishers, 1919; reissued by Arno, 1968). I found a good deal of relevant material in two excellent surveys of black history, John Hope Franklin, *From Slavery to Freedom* (New York: Knopf, 1947) and August Meier and Eliot M. Rudwick, *From Plantation to Ghetto* (New York: Hill and Wang, 1966). Henry Allen Bullock, *A History of Negro Education in the South: From 1619 to the Present* (Cambridge: Harvard University Press, 1967) provided some information; however, despite its title, only a few pages are devoted to the pre-Civil War period. One of the best discussions of Negro education in the antebellum North is found in Leon F. Litwack, *North of Slavery: The Negro in the Free States, 1790–1860* (Chicago: University of Chicago Press, 1961). Some interesting material on conditions of and attitudes toward schooling for blacks in Northern cities is contained in Gilbert

Osofsky, "The Enduring Ghetto," *The Journal of American History*, Vol. LV, No. 2 (Sept. 1968). A rich source of information for my discussion of Prudence Crandall comes from Edmund Fuller, *Prudence Crandall: An Incident of Racism in Nineteenth-Century Connecticut* (Middletown, Connecticut: Wesleyan University Press, 1971). A detailed study of Frederick Douglass's campaign against segregation in Rochester is Judith P. Ruchkin, "The Abolition of 'Colored Schools' in Rochester, New York, 1832–1856," *New York History*, Vol. LI, No. 4 (July 1970). Documents relating to the Roberts case and segregation in Boston are found in Daniel Calhoun (ed.), *The Educating of Americans: A Documentary History* (Boston: Houghton Mifflin, 1969).

*a chronology of
significant events
in the age of the
common school,
1830-1865*

1830 American Institute of Instruction founded in Boston
      Workingmen's parties adopted educational reform as a
      primary goal
1831 Nat Turner's uprising resulted in the intensification of
      efforts to prevent the education of Negroes in the South
      National American Lyceum organized
      First coeducational public high school established in
      Lowell, Massachusetts
1832 Prudence Crandall began her two-year struggle to
      maintain a seminary of black girls in Canterbury,
      Connecticut
1834 Pennsylvania School Law passed
1835 Thaddeus Stevens issued his famous defense of the
      school tax in Pennsylvania
      Local residents destroyed the integrated Noyes
      Academy at Canaan, New Hampshire
1836 Calvin Stowe commissioned by the Ohio legislature to
      examine and report on European schools (Report
      issued in 1837)
1837 Massachusetts established state Board of Education.
      Horace Mann appointed Secretary of the Board

"Stigma of Poverty" removed from the public schools
of Philadelphia

Samuel Lewis named Ohio's first state Superintendent of
Schools (office abolished in 1843, reestablished in 1853)

Massachusetts law passed requiring children to receive
schooling prior to employment in mills and factories

Michigan entered the Union with constitutional
provisions for state responsibility for promoting and
supervising public schools

1838   First state normal school opened at Lexington,
Massachusetts

Oberlin College inaugurated coeducation on the
collegiate level

Henry Barnard named Secretary of the Connecticut
Board of Education

1839   Catholic school controversy began in New York

Henry Barnard conducted nation's first teachers'
institute in Connecticut

Virginia Military Institute founded

1842   District common-school system extended to New York
City

Controversy over Bible reading and religious exercises
in the public schools of Philadelphia began

1843   Henry Barnard appointed agent for promoting public
education in Rhode Island

1844   Horace Mann's Seventh Annual Report embroiled him
in conflict with Boston schoolmasters

1847   Beginning of the Sheffield Scientific School at Yale

1848   First state reform school opened at Westborough,
Massachusetts

In the Roberts case Massachusetts Supreme Court
upheld Boston's right to maintain separate-but-equal
"colored" schools

1849   Avery College, first Negro sponsored college, founded.
Other Negro colleges of the period were Ashman
Institute (1854) and Wilberforce University (1855)

1851   Francis Wayland's experiment in college reform at

Brown University began

1852   Nation's first compulsory attendance law passed in Massachusetts

Boston Public Library founded

1854   Brooklyn Polytechnic Institute founded. Other significant scientific and technical institutions established during the era were Cooper Union (1859) and Massachusetts Institute of Technology (1865)

1855   Henry Barnard began editing his *American Journal of Education*

Free-school law passed in Illinois

Segregated schools barred by law in Massachusetts

St. Paul's School of Concord, New Hampshire founded

Mrs. Carl Shurz opened nation's first kindergarten in Watertown, Wisconsin. The language of instruction was German

1859   Elmira Female College became the first women's institution to grant B.A. degrees equivalent to those earned at respected men's colleges

1860   First English language kindergarten established in Boston by Elizabeth Peabody

1861   At Oswego, New York, Edward Sheldon inaugurated a teacher-training program stressing Pestalozzian principles

First schools for freed blacks in Union-occupied territory established at Alexandria and Fortress Monroe in Virginia

1862   Morrill Act passed by Congress establishing land-grant colleges

Washington, D.C. made its first provisions for Negro schooling

John Swett elected state Superintendent of Schools in California

1865   The Freedmen's Bureau was established, and the federal government assumed a major role in educating former slaves

index